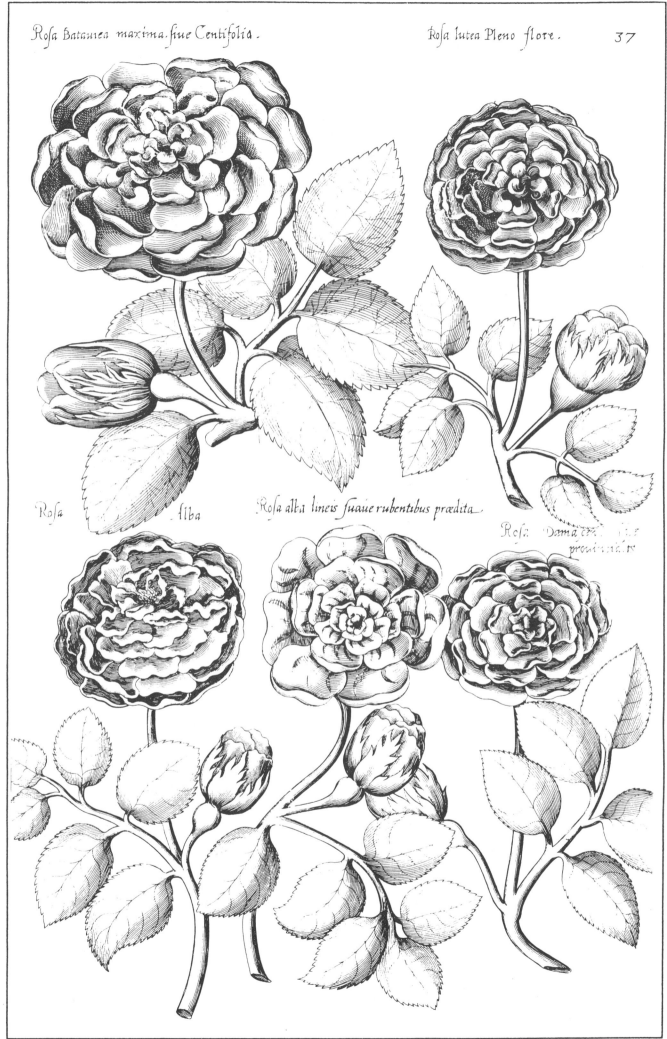

Rosa Batauea maxima, siue Centifolia.

Rosa lutea Pleno flore.

Rosa   Alba

Rosa alba lineis suaue rubentibus prædita.

Rosa Dama cena siue
prouincialis

Roses from Sweert's Florilegium (1612).

The Embroiderer's Flowers

Detail of a tent-stitch screen worked by Lady Julia Calverley in 1727. Baskets were favourite containers for flowers in the eighteenth century.

Janet Haigh's portrait of Miss Jekyll (1989) celebrates her love of needlework as well as her skill as a garden designer. Worked in coloured silks on a painted silk ground, it depicts one of her famous tonal borders, with flowers in drifts planted in 'graduated harmonies culminating into gorgeousness'.

THE EMBROIDERER'S FLOWERS

Thomasina Beck

We dream our dreams.
What should we be, without our fabulous flowers?
Vita Sackville-West, *The Garden.*

David & Charles

FOR CHRISTOPHER

PAGE 3
*In this drawing of the author's garden, Clare Roberts
emphasises the 'hint of ornament' in the stamens and
distinctive 'streamers' of Saxifraga fortunei which make
the plant such a perfect subject for embroidery.*

OPPOSITE
*Mirror frame c1650 with a squirrel, snails, butterflies and
flowers in needlelace stitches. Although flowers in dress were
out of fashion by this date, they frequently appear embroidered
on the gowns of the female figures in stumpwork.*

A DAVID & CHARLES BOOK

Copyright © Thomasina Beck 1992

First Published 1992

A catalogue record for this book is available from the British Library.

ISBN 0 7153-9901-2

Typset by ABM Typographics Ltd, Hull
and printed in The Netherlands by Roto Smeets Offset
for David & Charles
Brunel House   Newton Abbot   Devon

CONTENTS

French tapestry c1500, one of a set depicting scenes of
courtly life. The lady is engaged in embroidery, often
described as the art of the needle which clearly
distinguishes it from tapestry – woven on a loom.

CHAPTER HEADING
This woodcut from the Herbal of Tabernaemontanus (1588)
illustrates the new-found pleasure in cultivating flowers
and gardens in the sixteenth century, with ladies busy
watering and setting out plants in spring.

INTRODUCTION

In the Musée de Cluny in Paris hangs a mille fleur tapestry entitled 'Embroidery'. It depicts a lady seated in a flowery mead, a basket of threads by her side, her needle raised to complete the last stitches on the cushion in her lap. The needlework flowers echo those powdering the grass around her, just as they do in Botticelli's rendering of Flora in the *Primavera*, radiant in a flowing, flower-embroidered gown. These supremely romantic images bring alive the words of poets and writers past and present, when they compare the earth 'apparelled' with flowers to embroidery.

Motif of a pink from Flora's dress drawn by A. H. Christie (for an article on 'Floral Designs' in Embroidery, *1909)* *showing how flowers must be formalised to make effective embroidery patterns.*

This is how Chaucer conjures up the dazzling appearance of the young squire in the 'Prologue' to the *Canterbury Tales*:

Embroudered was he, as it were a mede,
Al ful of fresshe floures whyte and red.

The 'floures' on his short gown were daisies, Chaucer's favourite spring flower, which he would get up to admire at dawn in the first rays of sunlight on a May morning. The flowers symbolised his delight at the return of spring, and the embroidery recorded their freshness and gaiety.

Nearly six centuries later John Clare, the peasant poet, used a similar image:

Daisies ye flowers of lowly birth
Embroiderers of the carpet earth
That stud the velvet sod.

But for embroiderers perhaps the most telling comparison of all was made by Vita Sackville-West in her long poem *The Garden*, when she wrote:

Innumerable, the small flow'rs that stitch
Their needlework on canvas of the ground

She was thinking of Botticelli's flowers 'Small, brilliant, close to earth and youngly gay', pulsatillas, scillas and the wood anemone which transform the bleak wintry canvas with their brightness; but her verse also expresses the excitement embroiderers feel when they enrich and diversify a bare ground with the colours and textures of needlework, and gradually see the shapes and forms of flowers emerge.

In the past, the verb 'to flower' meant the same as to embroider, and for many people embroidery is still synonymous with flowers. The brilliance and sheen of silks, the varied textures of wools, linens and cottons, and the subtle intermingling of pearls and many-faceted beads, all seem made for recreating the flowers that give such pleasure in gardens, fields and hedgerows, or that are gathered for enjoyment indoors.

When we record this pleasure in needlework today we are following a tradition that stretches back in time far beyond

Simple 'powdering' designs for daisies by (left) Jacques Le Moyne de Morgues 1586, and (right) Joan Drew 1929.

7

the Cluny cushion. Embroidery is as old as the silks that are its glory – the earliest surviving example may well be a fragment which was found in the Caves of the Thousand Buddhas at Dunhuang on the ancient silk route from China, and whose silk flowers still glow in the dim light of the British Museum. I came on that fragment by chance, while waiting for a pattern book in the North Library.

I had been trying to make up my mind what scope my book should have. Should it be limited to the West, or should it try to encompass the East and the New World? Staring at the Chinese flowers worked twelve centuries ago, bemused and fascinated by their extreme age and continuing beauty, I found my answer in the questions the fragment posed. Who had made it, and what was its purpose? What flowers were they, and what was their significance? I reflected that each embroidery has its own story to tell, and if we are to learn something of interest and value about it, if it is to reveal something of its makers and their lives, then that story must be told slowly and in depth. The history of flowers in embroidery worldwide was far beyond the scope of a single volume.

I returned to the North Library and opened the copy of Jacques Le Moyne de Morgues' *La Clef des Champs* printed in 1586; I looked at the page where the small motifs of red and musk-roses, wild strawberries and stocks had been pricked round the outline to make patterns. I would begin here, in

SPRING·NEVER·DID·FORGET·
TO·BLESS·THE·YEAR·WITH·
BROIDERD·LOVELINESS·

Flowers for a spring sampler by Joan Drew, illustrated in The Embroidress *(1937).*

Detail of Botticelli's Primavera *(1478) showing Flora transformed by her flower-embroidered dress.*

The outline of the stock in this page from La Clef des Champs *has been pricked round ready for transferring the pattern to the ground.*

the sixteenth century in England, when the excitement and enthusiasm for flowers, and for rendering them in embroidery, was at fever pitch. It was then that our long-lasting affair with flowers and gardens really began, that some of the most imaginative and exquisite embroidery ever created was first seen and admired. The writers of those days knew that embroidery at first hand, and they wrote of the flowers that inspired it with deep affection and wit, and above all with wonder, so their prose is still exceptionally pleasurable to read; indeed, they often seemed to be exactly in tune with the embroiderers of their day:

> Into your garden you can walk
> And with the plants and flowers talk

suggests John Rea in *Flora* in 1660, and his words take us straight into the curious world of stumpwork where conversations between flowers, animals and people seem quite natural.

The history of embroidery is therefore firmly intertwined with that of flowers, but it is far less richly documented. Compared to the many botanists, herbalists, plant-hunters and garden-makers and writers who described their occupations with enthusiasm, few embroiderers wrote about their work or that of their contemporaries, their sources of inspiration or the books and materials they used. This makes the evidence of those few who did record their impressions especially valuable, and it explains why certain names – Mrs Delany in the eighteenth century, for example – recur so often in these pages. Some of her drawings are reproduced as well, but she was exceptional in her day in making up her own designs.

Until the twentieth century, few embroiderers were concerned if they were unable to draw and design their own patterns. Many found their inspiration in the limitless store of motifs in the herbals and beautiful illustrated flower books known as *florilegia*. They chose the simplest in outline, and the most decorative, and made them their own by thoughtful adaptation and personal choice of colours and stitches. In fact a surprising number of botanical artists intended their illustrations to be useful to embroiderers, and many examples of their work are reproduced here because they still seem to offer as much inspiration now as in the past.

Flower motifs from pattern books long out of print are also included, and suggestions for adapting them are made in each chapter. There are also suggestions as to how the flowers illustrated might be adapted for contemporary use in the embroidery of simple items for presents or personal use. I hope they may reawaken interest in some of the forgotten but wonderfully decorative needlework items of the past, like the book covers of the seventeenth century, and in methods such as blackwork and crewelwork.

William Morris drew his inspiration from real flowers, from herbals, and from old embroideries, particularly from crewelwork. A look at his designs shows how fruitful such sources can be. He modestly described himself as 'an ornamentalist, a maker of would-be pretty things'. How many embroiderers today would be happy to have as much said of them? The desire to create is strong in all of us, but the problem of finding the right motifs and devising patterns remains a real one. I hope this book will provide inspiration for all would-be makers of pretty things.

Jennifer Wilson's 'Daffodils and Grape Hyacinths' (1988) was inspired by a group of spring flowers in her cold Morayshire garden. Machine satin stitch conveys the flowing line of stems and foliage, contrasting well with the build-up of hand satin stitch in glossy silk used for the grape hyacinths.

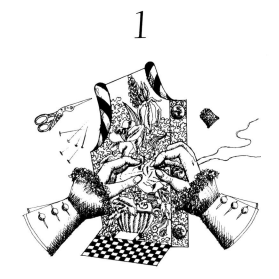

FLOWERS FOR DRESS

'A PARADICE OF FLOWERS'

The flowers, like brave embroidered girls,
Looked as they most desired . . .
Michael Drayton, 1606

Flowers have always been favourite motifs for dress the world over, but like all fashions, they are essentially ephemeral and regularly give way to other forms of decoration; until such time as they reappear transformed by different stitches and materials, or a different scale, or with a new choice of flowers to suit the taste of another age. Yet occasionally they remain in favour much longer, and this was what happened in Renaissance England when for nearly half a century, from the beginning of Queen Elizabeth I's reign until well into the seventeenth century, clearly recognisable pinks, roses and many other wild and garden flowers appeared and reappeared on the dress of ladies, gentlemen and children, intricately embroidered in silks and gold.

This vogue had no real counterpart on the Continent, and its long duration only makes sense when it is related to the extraordinary expansion of interest in flowers and gardens at that time.

'There is not almost one nobleman, gentleman or merchant that hath not great store of these flowers', wrote William Harrison in his *Description of England* in 1587. Native and foreign flowers were eagerly discussed and carefully cultivated by wealthy enthusiasts who vied with each other in displaying their collections, and similar competitive fervour inspired the followers of fashion when working out eye-catching floral schemes on their dress.

In that ambitious age appearance was all-important, and courtiers in search of royal favour endeavoured to stand out from the crowd by parading a succession of spectacular outfits demonstrating not only their status, but – just as important – their cultivated taste. Ostentatious spending of the family fortune was not enough to ensure success – the most diligent study of the cut, colour and textures of dress was also necessary, *and* evidence of artistic imagination in its

William Larkin's portrait of the 4th Earl of Dorset c1613, depicts the flowers on his costume in minutest detail. The pansy and rose heads are outlined in tiny pearls with gold beads at their centres, and these beads also form the strawberry seeds. The flowers are repeated not only on the shoes, but on each petal of the glittering spangled shoe 'roses'.

decoration. An anonymous verse from *A Poetical Rhapsody* (1602) sums up these modish aspirations to perfection:

> My love in her attire doth show her wit,
> It doth so well become her;
> For every season she hath dressings fit,
> For winter, spring, and summer.

The lines praise a lady, but they could equally well have been addressed to a fashionable gallant like Edward Sackville, 4th Earl of Dorset, who was esteemed for the beauty and grace of his person and for his sparkling wit. In William Larkin's portrait he wears the sumptuous costume probably designed and worn for the marriage of James I's daughter Princess Elizabeth to the Elector Palatine on Valentine's Day, 1613. He chose simple flowers treated with the utmost sophistication in terms of colour and texture: single red roses, wild strawberries and blue pansies sparkle and glow against the shimmering pale violet taffeta of the doublet and the refulgent black velvet of the breeches.

Flamboyant, elaborately co-ordinated schemes like Lord Dorset's mark the culmination of this long love affair with flowers on dress. It had begun far more simply, with the embroidery of favourite flowers such as carnations or columbines worked as a decorative finish round the neck and cuffs of fine white linen or cambric gentlemen's shirts and ladies' smocks, glimpsed beneath doublets and bodices in portraits and miniatures. The delicate flower patterns in blackwork (embroidery in black silks on a white ground) emphasised the snowy whiteness of the gossamer fine linen, and drew attention to ring-laden hands and carefully tended complexions. When he wrote the following little verse, perhaps Lord Dorset was thinking of the becoming effect of blackwork framing the face:

> Tell me Dorinda, why so gay?
> Why such embroidery fringe and lace?
> Can any dress find a way
> To stop the approaches of decay
> And mend a ruined face?

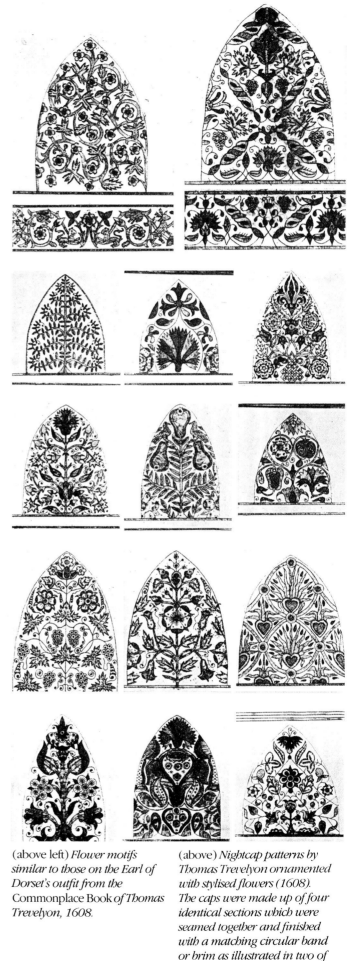

(above left) *Flower motifs similar to those on the Earl of Dorset's outfit from the* Commonplace Book of *Thomas Trevelyon, 1608.*

(above) *Nightcap patterns by Thomas Trevelyon ornamented with stylised flowers (1608). The caps were made up of four identical sections which were seamed together and finished with a matching circular band or brim as illustrated in two of the examples on this page.*

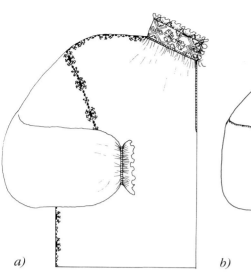

a)

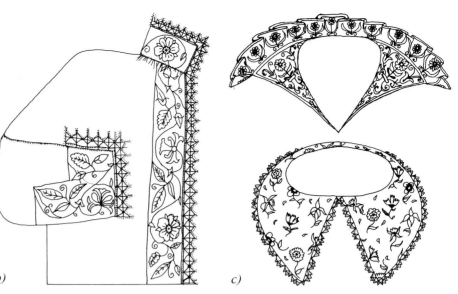

b)

c)

d)

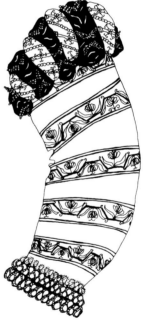

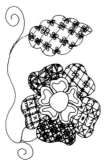

e)

Flowers in blackwork:
(a) A man's shirt c1540, worked with columbines in blue silk set in an interlace pattern.
(b) A man's shirt c1600 with a coiling stem or waved line pattern of roses and honeysuckle.
(c) A lady's collar c1540 and a child's collar c1590, worked with small sprigs of flowers.
(d) Detachable sleeves with flower patterns based on portraits (from left to right 1587, 1590, 1570, 1580) showing stylised flowers in band and coiling stem designs. Acorns, peapods, vines and pomegranates were often included with the flowers. The sleeves were attached to the bodice by decorative tags known as 'points'.
(e) The motifs in blackwork could either be worked in minute speckling stitches, or in tiny geometric patterns on the counted thread.

An anonymous portrait of a young man c1590, wearing a blackwork doublet veiled over the sleeves with transparent gauze. The tendrils and twining stems echo the honeysuckle and roses on the arbour.

Never has underwear been so charmingly ornamented; similar flowers also appeared on men's nightcaps, on ladies' caps known as coifs (see p127), on the triangular forehead cloths designed to be worn with them – to smooth out wrinkles, some used to say – on handkerchiefs and sleeves.

As the century progressed blackwork became ever more elaborate, spreading over stand-up and turn-down collars, and eventually covering the entire surface of voluminous sleeves and shirts, with exuberant designs of twisting stems enclosing large daffodils, pansies and many other favourites. Then, as the century drew to a close, these clearly recognisable flowers began to sport fanciful leaves and were joined by exotic unidentifiable blooms.

Twentieth-century eyes peering through a magnifying glass at these intricate flowers cannot fail to be amazed by the precision of the infinitesimally small stitches, and to marvel at the imaginative fancy which created such a 'paradice of dainty devices' within the compass of a single bloom. The effect of the finest black silk on cobweb lawn was of the utmost refinement; but when the same patterns were worked in glittering gold, with spangles and in brilliantly coloured silks, gaiety replaced sobriety, and the embroidery on jackets, stomachers, nightcaps and gloves took on a new and dazzling exuberance. This effect can be seen in the stitchery of a jacket owned by Margaret Laton, one of Queen Elizabeth's ladies-in-waiting: a bright miscellany of flowers all grow from the same golden stem, as if a magical plant harbouring birds, snails and butterflies, had spread over the spangle-strewn ground.

The same type of pattern was chosen by Elizabeth Vernon, another lady-in-waiting but one who in 1598 had incurred Queen Elizabeth's displeasure by her marriage to

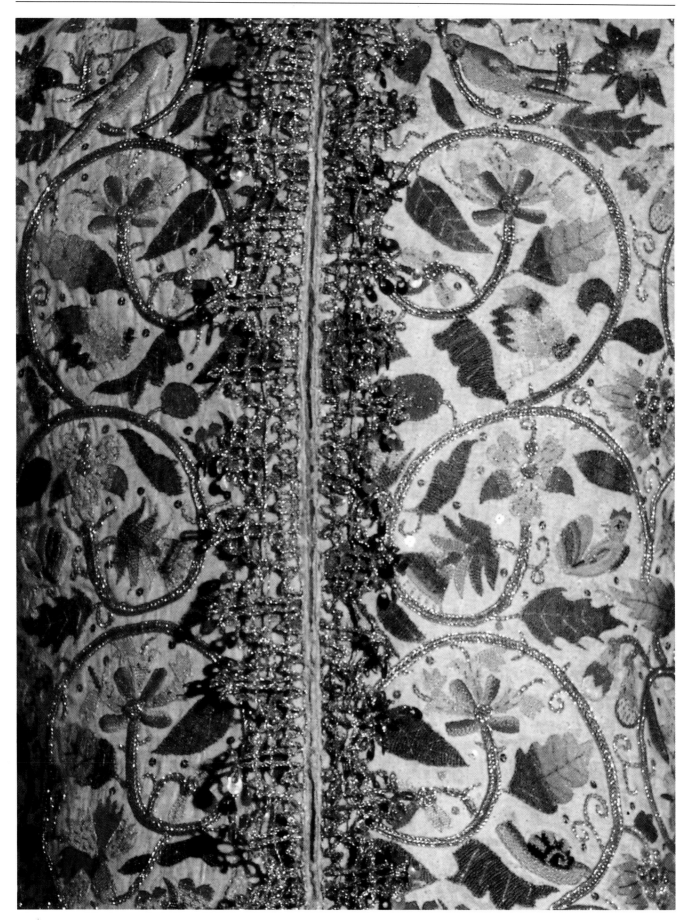

Margaret Laton's jacket, c1610.
The coiling stems are in
interlaced braid stitch with
tendrils in chain stitch.

Shakespeare's staunch friend and patron the 3rd Earl of Southampton. The wedding may have been the occasion for which *A Midsummer Night's Dream* was written, and it is tempting to speculate whether Shakespeare had seen her wearing the dress in the portrait, and if so whether he had her, Titania-like, in mind in such phrases as 'starlit spangled sheen' (Act I, Sc II) which sum up so marvellously the enchantment and glamour of Elizabethan dress. On her jacket the flowers are realistically shaded, suggesting professional expertise: indeed, they might have been stitched by an embroiderer such as the one described in the anonymous play *Sir Giles Goosecap* (1606) who could work 'any flower to the life as like as if it grew in the very place'.

The counterplay between real and imaginary pervaded literature and all the arts in Shakespearean England. It appears at its most intriguing in floral dress embroidery,

when real flowers – single pinks or nosegays – and their jewelled counterparts in the shape of brooches and necklaces (like the ornament of enamelled daisies displayed on the curtain in Elizabeth Vernon's portrait) were pinned to bodices ornamented with needlework flowers. The embroidered blooms were doubly fascinating, as they echoed both the brilliance of the jewelled flowers and the freshness of the living ones (see p114), and they were admired as much for their artifice as for their lifelike appearance.

Margaret Laton and Elizabeth Vernon could very well have bought their jackets ready-made in the smart shops in Cheapside or the fashionable Royal Exchange. Once there, they might have lingered to examine the milliner's stock of flower-embroidered gloves, coifs, sweet bags and nightcaps, all of which made excellent presents.

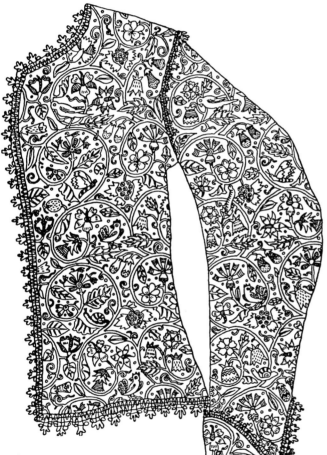

a)

b)

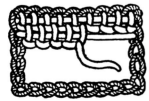

c)

(a) The design on Margaret Laton's jacket was drawn for an article in Embroidery, 1909 by Grace Christie. (b) The detail shows the stems in braid stitch and the leaves in detached buttonhole stitch. (c) Detached buttonhole stitch is worked over laid threads within a chain outline (see also p14). (d) Spiderweb stitch forms the centre of the honeysuckle on the jacket.

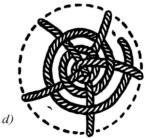

d)

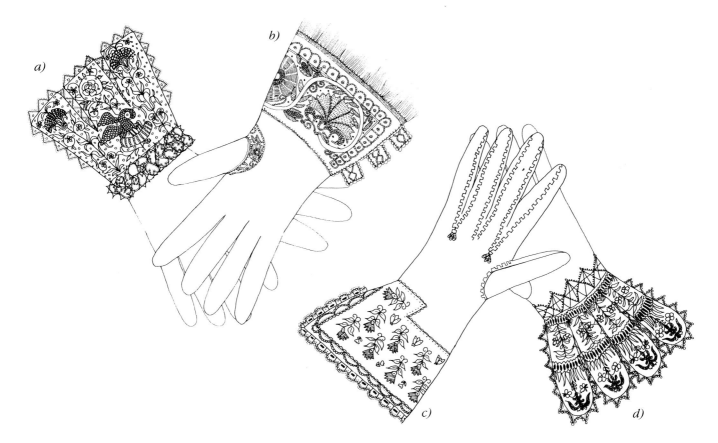

a) *b)*

c) *d)*

Except for gloves, many of these items were also worked at home, and the Exchange was the place to buy threads and materials. Extravagantly embroidered gloves were designed and made by professionals, not for warmth and protection, but entirely for display. They were totally unpractical, and were worn as a symbol of rank and leisure to impress the beholder, and to make it clear that the wearer had no need to lift the proverbial finger, but had donned them merely for the sake of elegance. They were esteemed as gifts, and were often presented in boxes perfumed – to match their contents – with white jasmine and roses. The pedlar Autolycus in *A Winter's Tale* sold 'gloves as sweet as Damask roses'; these might have been embroidered, but they were more likely to have been scented ones which lovers would exchange as a token, or which a bridegroom would offer to the wedding guests. Many gloves were lavishly trimmed with metal lace, and this trimming was also used for the showy 'roses' on shoes, charmingly described in this popular verse:

> When roses in the garden grew,
> And not in ribbons on a shoe,
> Now ribbon roses take their place
> Then garden roses want their grace.

Presentation gloves with richly embroidered gauntlets: (a) white satin encrusted with metal threads, (b) carnations in tiny pearls on a coiling stem repeated in miniature round the thumb, (c) small sprigs with further decoration emphasising the long fingers, (d) bands of flowers repeated in the tabs. Small gussets between the tabs enabled the gauntlet to flare out over the wearer's sleeve and cuff.

Moreover, when silver and gold spangles were sewn to the lace, the resemblance to a real rose glistening with dew was even more apparent. Hamlet (Act III Sc II) mentions the two 'provincial roses on my razed shoes', and was doubtless thinking of the many-layered effect of the double Provins rose.

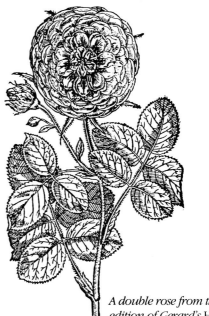

A double rose from the 1633 edition of Gerard's Herball.

(left) Elizabeth Vernon, Countess of Southampton, c1600. This anonymous portrait shows how a fashionable costume was put together with miscellaneous items; it took considerable care and time to pin and lace these together, hence the remark in Tomkis' play Lingua *'A ship is sooner rigged by far, than a gentlewoman made ready'. The lifelike flowers on the jacket contrast with the more stylised sprigs on the skirt.*

A sweet bag, c1600, embroidered with flowers raised in detached buttonhole stitch on a coiling stem of interlaced braid stitch, trimmed with matching tassels.

The Penn Purse, a wallet worked with motifs in tent stitch on a silver ground. It was made for Admiral Sir William Penn whom Pepys described as 'a hypocritical rogue' and

'jovial rascall, fond of his glass, and telling a good story, or singing a song, quite uninterested by any puritanical scruples'.

a)

b)

c)

d)

Flower-ornamented sweet bags: (a) worked with seed pearls on red satin and a matching knife case, (b) borage and rose sprigs, their stiff leaves emphasising the diagonals of

the interlace design, (c) roses and a carnation crowned head, (d) a coiling stem design with the pink repeated on the matching pincushion.

In 1614 the Earl of Northampton's inventory listed twelve sweet bags, one of which was 'embrodered with a running worke of roses and flowers in silke and golde'; it was lined with striped silk and probably resembled the enchanting example illustrated. Like the gloves, these delectable items were not intended for everyday use but were exchanged as gifts, made all the more desirable when they contained money, perfumes or sweetmeats. Many of these purses have a jewelled quality, with sparkling flowers on a gold or silver-gilt tent-stitch or gobelin-stitch ground, and all are exquisitely finished with hand-made cords, tassels, or ornamental knobs.

A fascinating late example was made for Admiral Sir William Penn (1621–70) after whom Pennsylvania was named. This swashbuckling character captured Jamaica in 1659 and returned in triumph in 1660 to be knighted by Charles II. The purse was made to celebrate the event, and depicts the Admiral resplendent in lace-trimmed breeches and bucket boots, flanked by an outsize cornflower and a parrot on a cherry sprig; however, there is no trace of floral ornament on his stylish dress. Even his sash, one of the last accessories to be decorated with flowers, is plain.

It is interesting that at the battle of Edgehill in 1642 Charles I wore a deep violet military sash embroidered with carnations, roses and tulips in a tracery of silver – a poignant survivor, not only of the battle, but of this exceptionally long-lasting fashion for flower embroidery. By 1625 when he came to the throne, lustrous unadorned satins were already replacing the former riot of floral decoration, and such extravagance became totally inappropriate during the Commonwealth.

'FLOWERS IN THEIR NATURAL COLOURS'

After nearly a century's absence from fashion, flower-embroidered dress was welcomed back in the eighteenth century, and worn with panache at the courts of George I and George II. In 1739, Mrs Delany, an inveterate party-goer and a witty and opinionated correspondent, was a guest at a ball given by Frederick, Prince of Wales, and made a particular note of the abundance of embroidery, 'the men as fine as the women'. On occasions such as this the most elaborate finery was essential, and embroidery assured the wearer of a certain exclusivity; the aim, as in the past, was to dazzle and impress, not only by the obvious expense incurred, but by eye-catching and often idiosyncratic floral designs.

Of all the sumptuous outfits on display that evening in 1739, Mrs Delany was especially impressed by the green silk petticoat sparkling with cornflowers and rococo motifs in silver and gold worn by the Duchess of Bedford, and the white satin gown worked with 'flowers in their natural colours' over rich gold net chosen by the Princess of Wales. As she was herself a keen and accomplished embroiderer, her comments on the subject are particularly interesting. Mrs Delany was born in 1700 and died in 1788, and during her long life she recorded her own and her friends' needlework in her letters and diaries. She could easily differentiate

between professional and domestic work, and had decided views on what constituted good and bad taste in the choice of designs and colour schemes.

At the prince's ball the following year she dismissed the clumsy festoons on Lady Scarborough's petticoat as *nothing at alls supported by pillars*, reserving her praise for the truly astonishing outfit worn by the Duchess of Queensberry. This was in white satin ornamented with nasturtiums, convolvulus and other twining plants, their leaves so enlivened by gold thread that they '... looked like the gilding of the sun. I never saw a piece of work so prettily fancied', she wrote, 'and am quite angry with myself for not having the same thought, for it is infinitely handsomer than mine, and could *not* cost *much more.*'

Sketches of flowers made by Mrs Delany.

Mrs Delany was exceptional in devising her own patterns, not only for small items like handkerchiefs and aprons, but also for something as complicated as the elaborate court dress she embroidered. We can still see parts of the petticoat and gown (see illustration p77) and admire her beautiful stitchery of mixed flowers, where she uses bright twisted silks rather than the expensive gold threads preferred by the Duchess of Queensberry. It would be interesting to have her comments on a particularly spectacular gown in the Victoria and Albert Museum, as the jasmine and convolvulus at the top of the skirt are quite amateurishly worked in comparison to the crisp professionalism of the rococo

Gown in the rococo style (1744) embroidered in long and short stitch and French knots in coloured silks and silver with poppies, auriculas, anemones, roses and honeysuckle.

that different hands were engaged on it. In professional workrooms, then as now, the material was mounted on a frame so that more than one embroiderer could work on it at the same time, and this might explain the inconsistency. However, the dress was made in 1744 for the wedding of Isabella Courtenay, daughter of Sir William Courtenay, and the embroidery for such an important commission would surely have been strictly supervised. There is a more sentimental theory that the bride and her sisters wanted to demonstrate their needlework skills in completing the flowers and perhaps this is the right one. In 1797 Queen Charlotte told Fanny Burney how her daughter, the Princess Royal, had worked her own wedding dress without any help at all 'well knowing that 3 stitches done by any other would make it immediately said it was none of it by herself'. In Mrs Delany's opinion ladies' needlework ought to be superior to bought work in design and taste, and their plain sewing 'a model for their maids'.

This was certainly true of the heroine, Clarissa, in Samuel Richardson's popular novel *Clarissa: a History of a Young Lady* (1744). She was an arbiter of local fashion and a fine needlewoman, and in the story she is described by her admirer Lovelace as wearing a dress of pale primrose silk 'the cuffs and robings curiously embroidered by the ever-charming Arachne, in a running pattern of violets and leaves; the ourselves how captivating she looked from Francis Hayman's painting, which depicts her abduction by Lovelace.

The embroidery on formal gowns and petticoats was seen to best advantage when the skirt was supported by a hooped petticoat worn beneath it; however, the wearer's appearance was less impressive when she sat down in a chair and was 'hid up to her ears on either side like a swan with her head between lifted wings' – in the words of a sketch writer in *The Gentleman's Magazine* of 1750. To fold or collapse the hoops – essential for getting into a sedan chair – the wearer could reach down through the placket holes let into the top seam of the skirt; these were also the way into a pair of pockets, concealed beneath the skirt and attached by tapes tied round the waist. It was not until the 1790s that ladies' handbags, or 'indispensables' appeared; until then such pockets were invaluable for carrying about small essential items and money – a fact well known to the pickpockets of the day, some of whom specialised in whipping them off!

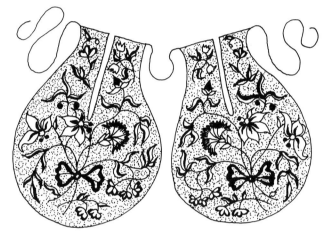

A pair of pockets with central openings ornamented with lilies and carnations on linen, worked with a vermicular pattern in running stitch.

They were often embroidered with small flower sprays or twining stems in silks and crewels, and similar decoration was popular on the night and morning caps designed for men, where a meandering pattern in flat quilting might enhance the flowers and help to strengthen and shape the cap.

Detail from 'The Abduction of Clarissa' by Francis Hayman. Petticoats could either match or contrast with the gown in colour and embroidery. Here the artist has added a band of violets to the yellow silk petticoat to match those on the stomacher and robings, or revers, on either side of it.

A man's nightcap designed for relaxing at home when the wig was removed. These caps were worn with a 'banyan', a grand but informal dressing gown, made in bright flowered satins and brocades whose lively colours harmonised with the flowers on the caps.

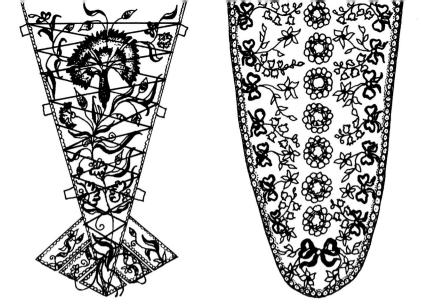

The triangular shape of the stomacher was well suited to branching sprays or loosely tied posies of flowers. The tabs were for pinning it to the corset and were hidden by the robings or revers of the gown. The stomacher (right) was designed by Mrs Delany for her court dress, and worked with carnation heads and alternating lily-of-the-valley and jasmine on black velvet.

This kind of decoration was also ideal for stiffening stomachers which, like pockets and caps, were sufficiently small in scale for the less ambitious embroiderer to tackle. Stomachers were essentially showy, designed to draw attention to a narrow waist and a fine décolletage, and the grandest glittered with encrustations of gold and silver flowers. The making of these was best left to the professionals, who specialised in using a great variety of metal threads: tinsel, coloured foil which could be cut into the shape of leaves, and paillettes, which resembled sequins and were available in countless sizes and shapes, some of them like diminutive flower-heads. The paillettes were often sewn on in overlapping lines with pieces of purl (tightly coiled gold wire) between each, and by varying the size, the most magical flowers, leaves and twisting stems could be created.

The sparkling purl would reflect on the paillettes like a myriad tiny mirrors, and the vibrating light of the thousands of candles normally used to illuminate important occasions would have intensified the shimmering effect.

The lure of such materials was hard to resist and the domestic embroiderer would try them out on decorative aprons, ornamenting these with flamboyant chinoiserie blooms, and using patterned leaves and petals in unlikely and scintillating colour contrasts. Real flowers, shaded in a naturalistic way, were included in some amateur work, but the results often looked spindly compared to the luxuriant, even strident examples embroidered by the professionals on the brightest imaginable silks and taffetas. Yet in complete contrast to these there were also long aprons flowered most delicately in whitework on fine lawn and muslin.

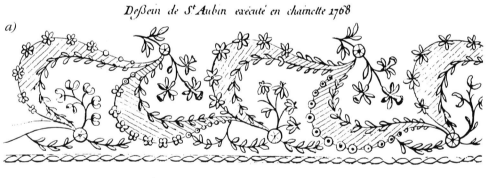

Deßein de Sᵗ Aubin executé en chainette 1768

a)

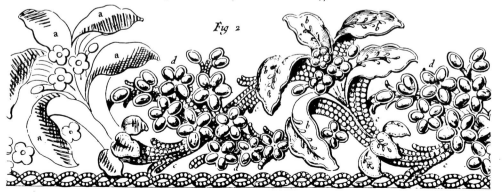

b)

Habit pour Mᵍʳ le Comte de Provence 1770.

Fig 2

Floral patterns from C. G. Saint-Aubin's L'Art du Brodeur (1770), showing (a) the use of paillettes in increasing size, and (b) flower petals outlined and veined in gold wire.

(right) An embroidery workroom from Diderot's Encyclopédie (1762). The girl is demonstrating a waistcoat pattern marked out and mounted on a frame. The other girl is at work by the window with paillettes, scissors and thread at hand.

Decorative aprons trimmed with metal lace and worked in bright colours and gilt threads on contrasting silk or satin grounds often had prettily scalloped edges echoing the curves of stems and leaves.

Printed designs for these, and for handkerchiefs, waistcoats and other items, began appearing as a feature in *The Lady's Magazine* from the 1770s and the dainty sprigs and trailing stems reflect the trend for lighter decoration in the latter part of the century. They were ideal for tambour work, in which a small hook was used to create quick regular chain stitch; this was the method chosen by Lady Ossory when in 1775 she made a waistcoat ornamented with roses for her friend Horace Walpole. Thanking her rapturously, he declared that such work 'came from no mortal hand'.

A pattern suitable for whitework from The Lady's Magazine, *1785.*

The waistcoat was the most lavishly embroidered item of a man's dress, and throughout the eighteenth century they were flowered with endlessly varied and wonderfully imaginative designs. Gay in crewelwork; elegant and refined in corded quilting, combined with pulled work and French knots; and seductive in coloured silks, the flowers were skilfully arranged in matching borders with the motifs ingeniously adapted to fit the pockets. The grandest were made to co-ordinate with dress suits in silks and velvets as splendidly decorated as any lady's gown. The cut and style of the flowers altered with succeeding seasons, their sophistication reaching an apogée towards the end of the century.

The formal suits of this period were made up in sumptuous patterned velvets, shot silks and brocades, with waistcoats often in a paler shade or in cream. None is perhaps better known than the outfit made by the Tailor of Gloucester for the Mayor's wedding on New Year's Day: the 'coat of cherry-coloured corded silk embroidered with pansies and roses', and the cream-coloured satin waistcoat trimmed with gauze and 'green worsted chenille' worked with poppies and cornflowers. Beatrix Potter modelled the mayor's outfit on a real coat and waistcoat in the Victoria and Albert Museum, and her illustrations capture to perfection the subtle nuances of shading and the sophisticated counterplay of colours, with the cherry-red of the coat repeated in the buttonholes of the waistcoat, completed at the last moment by the mouse embroiderer.

'SWEET LITTLE BUTTERCUP'

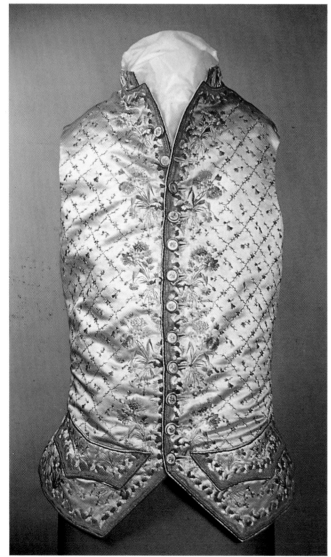

At the end of the eighteenth century flowers made a last appearance, in white on the white of soft muslin high-waisted gowns, worked with delicate borders of long trailing flowers which emphasised the new elongated line. After centuries of tight corseting these simple flowing dresses offered a delicious freedom, and it is easy to see why they were taken up yet again almost a century later during the aesthetic movement, as a healthy and elegant alternative to the rigid tight corseting of high fashion which was at its most absurdly restrictive during the 1870s and 1880s.

This novel type of dress can be seen in Thomas Armstrong's painting 'Haytime' exhibited at the Royal Academy in 1868. Despite their aprons, the trio are not haymakers but women wearing the most up-to-the-minute 'artistic' dress. Two of the dresses are lightly embroidered with flower patterns inspired by earlier crewelwork; in particular their loose cut is in striking contrast to the style of the time as depicted in the curvaceous silhouette and simpering posture of 'Sweet Little Buttercup' drawn by Linley Sambourne for *Punch* in 1879. Here the cartoonist makes fun both of the 'mermaid' line corset of high fashion and of the cult for Art Needlework (see Chapter 2) in which wild flowers such as buttercups and daisies were favourites.

The scissors by Buttercup's toes lie open on a William Morris pattern designed for the Royal School of Art Needlework, together with threads for working it. Morris's treatment of flowers – many of them wild rather than garden

24

...watercolour in the 'Tailor of Gloucester' was modelled on this waistcoat, c1775–80, worked with a trellis pattern enclosing tiny sprigs.

(left) 'Haytime' by Thomas Armstrong. The girls' 'artistic' appearance prompted the art critic in The Owl to describe them as 'three very plain persons who, having evidently not made hay while the sun shone, are now doing it by moonlight'.

"SWEET LITTLE BUTTERCUP;"
OR, ART-EMBROIDERY, 1879.

THE TIDY COSTUME.
A HINT TO ART NEEDLEWORKERS.

'Sweet Little Buttercup', a Punch cartoon mocking Art Needlework.

Punch's Almanach for 1880 makes fun of the aesthetic vogue and its symbol the sunflower. 'They look as if they had taken their curtains and

table covers and made them into a garment' was how a critic in Sylvia's Home Help Series described this type of dress.

'The Maid' in William Morris's
The Wood beyond the World
drawn by Edward Burne-Jones.

favourites – had started the cult, but it is hard to imagine anything further from his ideal of beautiful dress than this cartoon. He loved the flattering draperies worn by the saints in medieval illuminations and vestments, and figures like Flora in Botticelli's *Primavera*. His wife Janey's flowing gowns were reminiscent of these, and he begged women not to let themselves 'be upholstered like armchairs'.

Morris was fascinated by the power of Flora to transform the earth with her embroidery, and in his *Flora* tapestry of 1884 he depicts the goddess encircled with pinks and roses. Above her are the words:

> I am the handmaid of the earth
> I broider fair her glorious gown.

Was it Flora's glorious gown in the *Primavera* that inspired his description of the 'enchantress Maid' in his early romance *The Wood beyond the World*? In the story, the hero Walter and the Maid pause in a glade in the course of their flight, and the Maid loops garlands of roses and eyebright round her waist and coat. Walter fears the 'flowery array' will soon be faded, but the Maid's magical power refreshes them. When this power finally leaves her, Morris describes how her 'coat was now embroidered with the imagery of blossoms in silk gold and gems', suggesting that he thought of embroidery as a kind of magic which could make flowers immortal.*

*Joan Edwards in *Crewel Embroidery in England* (1975).

Nowhere (1891) when he describes a haymaking scene remembered from his boyhood, in which the bright embroidery on the girls' dresses transformed the meadow into a 'gigantic tulip bed'. In fact when *News from Nowhere* appeared, dresses with simple flower patterns round the neck and cuffs were already available from the well-known London shop Liberty's, which in 1884 had opened a special department for 'artistic and historic dress'. Earlier in the nineteenth century, the embroidery machine, invented in 1829, had caused much excitement with its ability to endlessly reproduce the most perfect blooms in satin stitch in shaded silks; but as the century drew to a close hand embroidery once again came to be appreciated as something precious and personal. In contrast to commercially made dresses it was also inexpensive – anyone using good but simple materials could follow Morris's idea of 'gardening with silk and gold thread' on ordinary garments that were easy to wear *and* beautiful. Early in the twentieth century, therefore, Liberty's also began to supply transfers for those who wanted to embroider and make their own clothes at home.

Morris's daughter May shared her father's interest in the needlework of the past, and her dress designs look back to the Elizabethan coiling stems and delicate patterns of the eighteenth century. She believed design to be 'the very soul and essence of beautiful embroidery'; the ornament she worked on the bodice of a blue serge dress (below) shows how effective the simplest treatment of flowers can be.

Although flowers came and went into and out of fashion many times during the twentieth century, they were never again to enjoy the long periods of popularity they had known in the sixteenth and eighteenth centuries. Nonetheless, highly stylised roses and leaves on collars and belts lent distinction to the otherwise simple dresses worn by Jessie Newbery and Ann Macbeth at the Glasgow School of Art at the turn of the century (see pp30 and 152 for their designs), and a succession of bewitching silk flowers adorned exquisitely fragile Edwardian tea gowns. The sinuous stems of Art

Bodice of a blue serge dress designed, worked and worn by May Morris. 'Of the colours principally used for embroidery', she wrote in

Decorative Needlework *'blue is one of the pleasantest ... choose those shades that have the pure, slightly grey tone of indigo dye.'*

Nouveau snaked about in satin stitch, and burst into exotic bloom in appliqué; beaded flowers shimmered on 'twenties' frocks, to be followed by chic stylised blooms in Art Deco patterns.

In Paris the embroidery house of Albert Lesage, founded in 1922, interpreted the changing designs of the couturiers with extraordinary panache, creating in beads, sequins, ribbons and threads of all kinds not only the textures and colours of flowers, but something of their essence as well. Of these perhaps the most remarkable adorn the jackets embroidered for Schiaparelli (including one she wore herself, ornamented with a glittering vine applied to brown velvet), and the dazzling iris and sunflower jackets designed by Yves St Laurent.

These were inspired by Vincent Van Gogh's celebrated paintings and were interpreted by Lesage in sequins, some set at an angle to catch and reflect the light thus building up a marvellously intricate surface. Of all the embroiderer's materials, beads and sequins create the most glamorous and spellbinding effects when applied to dress. François Lesage likens them to the brushes and paints of the artist – and they must be used with an artist's eye and sensitivity if they are to delight rather than overpower both the wearer and the beholder.

In its virtuoso technique and sophistication, the sunflower jacket is a gorgeous descendant of the flower-embroidered dress worn by the Earl of Dorset at the beginning of this chapter, by Queen Elizabeth (see p114) and by Isabella Courtenay (see p20). Like Flora's gown in the *Primavera* these are works of art whose romantic allure depends in no small measure on the magical effects of embroidery.

Jacket inspired by Van Gogh's sunflowers and iris designed by Yves St Laurent in 1987.

The intricate patterning of sunflowers is brilliantly conveyed in this detail of the beading by Lesage for the sunflower jacket.

Basia Zarzycka uses a rich palette of beads, crystals and fragments of antique textiles and lace in these shoes (1990), inspired by eighteenth-century models. She wanted to recreate the luxuriant 'garden' effect of rococo dress.

SOME VERY SIMPLE DESIGNS

The flowers and designs illustrated in this chapter can be adapted quite easily for contemporary use; children's dress in particular, being small in scale and uncomplicated in cut, invites this kind of ornament. Decoration on the yoke or round the hem and cuffs of a small girl's dress can transform it into something unique, and does not require a large repertoire of stitches. Many embroiderers today keep up to date with the latest techniques, and explore the potential of new materials without ever putting them to use in stitchery of a lasting kind. This seems to me a great pity when such pleasure and satisfaction can be derived from devising and working some decoration which the wearer as well as the worker will enjoy.

Choose a material which feels pleasant in the hand and is firm but soft in texture. Avoid anything flimsy, and make sure it will wash before devoting time to the embroidery. Children look well in dark as well as pale shades, and bright contrasting colours show up effectively when embroidered on deep blue, green and red grounds.

The decoration on the girls' dresses illustrated was chosen because it was so easy and quick to do. The tulip and daisies are in appliqué, and the leaf pattern is laid down in narrow braid. This kind of outline embroidery also looks effective in stem or chain stitch, especially the 'magic' variation of chain stitch or chequered chain in which two contrasting coloured threads are used.

An excellent pattern to start with is the waved line (familiar from the blackwork designs on p12), and some pretty examples based on leaf forms are illustrated in Joan Drew's *Embroidery and Design* (1929) – her clear, firmly drawn designs are exceptionally appealing. She often combines waved band patterns with straight lines, which she considered the 'foundation, support and scaffolding' in the building up of decorative designs; and in one chapter (entitled 'Some very simple designs, and how to draw them out on children's frocks') she explains how a variety of patterns can be developed from the simplest waved line, leading to more complex designs which can be either free and flowing or more geometric in character.

Unless you have experience in pattern-cutting, it is best to choose a paper pattern onto which you can transfer your chosen design. A photocopying machine can enlarge and reduce it so you can adapt the scale to fit the various pieces of yoke, cuffs and skirt; and a computer will solve the tricky problem of turning corners, always such a bugbear for embroiderers in the past – though it is worth remembering that some of their endeavours to solve the problem produced the most inventive and endearing solutions, as you can see in Mary Hulton's cushion with its waved band flower border illustrated on p37.

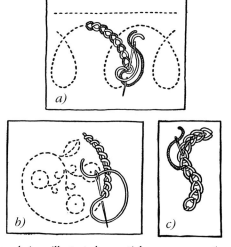

These designs illustrated an article on ornamenting children's dress in Aglaia, *the Journal of the Healthy and Artistic Dress Union (1893–4). The diagrams for (a) chequered (b) twisted and (c) back-stitched chain stitch are by Grace Christie.*

a)

b) ▲
▼

c)

Patterns for children's frocks based on waved line, leaf and simple flower motifs by Joan Drew: (a) the simplest variations on a waved line (b) borders built up with lines and ornaments (c) one leaf used in the composition of several designs, and (d) small units which, repeated, make effective borders.

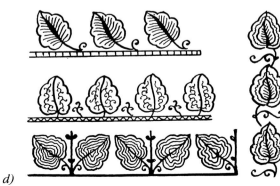

d)

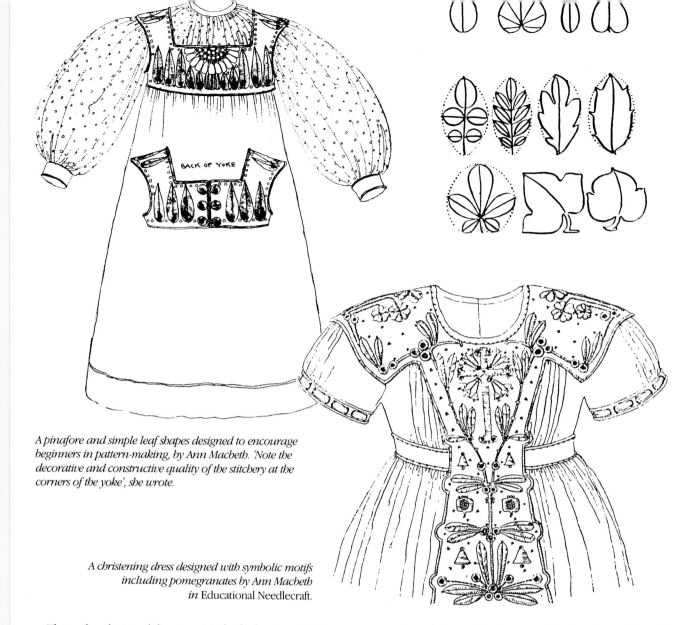

A pinafore and simple leaf shapes designed to encourage beginners in pattern-making, by Ann Macbeth. 'Note the decorative and constructive quality of the stitchery at the corners of the yoke', she wrote.

A christening dress designed with symbolic motifs including pomegranates by Ann Macbeth in Educational Needlecraft.

The yoke designed by Ann Macbeth for the pinafore described in *Educational Needlecraft* (1912) is ornamented with leaves of the simplest shape arranged with a large flower head, to be worked – like the collars and belts she devised for herself – in appliqué. 'Always draw in the main vein or "backbone" of a leaf first when designing it', she wrote, 'thus to gain a sure way of seeing that such leaves take the right direction and grow beautifully out of their stem lines if they have any.'

This is sound advice, as you will see if you try cutting some basic leaf shapes in paper and arranging them in groups or waved lines on the pattern pieces. Bold outlines like these also lend themselves to flat and shadow quilting on the yoke and as a border round the hem. A short quilted waistcoat could be made to co-ordinate with the dress, varying the colours and motifs in the manner of the eighteenth-century waistcoats. These are rich in inspiration, not only in the most imaginative floral patterning, but in unusual colour harmonies and combinations of stitches. What could be nicer

than a cherry-coloured waistcoat quilted with a trellis and sprig design drawn from the Tailor of Gloucester's outfit, and worn over a cream-coloured dress with larger sprigs set in a row along the yoke and hem?

Further inspiration might be found in the ravishingly pretty embroidered waistcoat buttons, which often repeated the motifs on an outfit on a smaller scale; typical examples can be seen on the ribbonwork waistcoat pictured on p83. Furthermore, narrow ribbons and ribbon-like threads are now available again in a variety of shades and surely rival the China ribbons of the nineteenth century; these could be used in sprig, flower-head and leaf patterns to create an attractive, easily rendered raised effect which would look equally good in bright fresh colours on a bridesmaid's dress or in white on white on a christening robe.

Waistcoat, drawn, painted and machine embroidered by Paddy Killer, 1991, and inspired by eighteenth-century waistcoats in the Laing Art Gallery, Newcastle upon Tyne, and botanical illustrations.

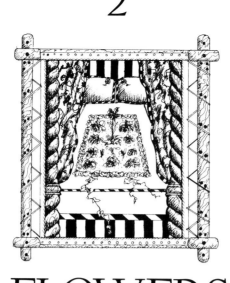

FLOWERS
FOR FURNISHING

'A THOUSAND FRAGRANT POSIES'

And I will make thee beds of roses,
And a thousand fragrant posies,
A cap of flowers and a kirtle,
Embroidered all with flowers of myrtle.
'The Passionate Shepherd to his Love',
Christopher Marlowe, 1589.

'Beds of roses' were no mere poet's fancy, but a reality in many of the fine new houses built in Marlowe's day. Furniture was sparse, and solid rather than comfortable, and the embroidered furnishings on beds, tables, chairs and stools transformed the interiors with colour and texture, making them more luxurious than ever before. Carpets (for the table rather than the floor), cushions, covers and, most eye-catching of all, elaborate bed-hangings were lavishly embroidered with the flowers of 'a thousand posies', and they brought the patterns and plants of the garden indoors in a most appealing way.

The flowers were worked in a great variety of methods,

and the stitches, colours and materials were most poetically described in wills and inventories. In 1585 for example, 'a carpet of needlework of sundrye coloured silkes . . . with a border of roses and sundrye posies about it' was listed in the Earl of Leicester's inventory. Most table carpets were worked in tent or cross stitch on linen which was long-lasting and produced a pleasing uniform effect. Lord Leicester's could have been stitched like this, or the motifs could have been outlined in heavy gold thread, or applied as slips, a favourite method at the time.

A slip was the name given to a detached motif whose outline was marked out in ink on linen, prior to being worked with silk or wool in tent stitch; it was then cut out and applied to a ground of satin or velvet. Mary Queen of Scots worked a number of these 'little flowers on canvas' when she was imprisoned at Lochleven. She clearly enjoyed this method since, nineteen years later . . . '52 different flowers in petit point [tent stitch] drawn from nature' were listed among the unfinished items in the inventory of her possessions at Chartley in 1586, the year before her death.

Part of an unfinished cushion cover c1600 similar in design to the chair cover illustrated (see p33). The flowers are set in an interlacing pattern of strawberries within a coiling stem border of borage and roses.

A lady of the Byng family attributed to Marcus Gheeraerts the Younger, c1618. The chair is worked with slips in an interlace pattern, and the table carpet with a flame design. Note the garden knots in the background.

Slips worked in tent stitch on linen ready to cut out and apply. The carnation is depicted with a heel exactly as if it were a gardener's slip or cutting.

(below) Formalised flower slips from a late sixteenth-century cushion.

(right) Slips from Richard Shorelyker's A Scholehouse for the Needle (1632).

'Spring at Hampton Court' by Vicky Lugg, 1990. A modern interpretation of a flower-filled knot inspired by the Tudor Garden at Hampton Court using two weights of painted canvas. The flowers are worked over the coarser of the two so that strips of fabric as well as threads can build up contrasts of texture.

Alternatively a small area was worked round the individual flowers, and these would then be mounted as small panels for wall- or bed-hangings. Framed with braid or cord, the effect was bold and striking, as for example in the octagonal and cruciform panels worked by Mary Queen of Scots and Bess of Hardwick, now at Oxburgh Hall. Sometimes the slips were set in the spaces of a knot or an interlace design identical to those laid out in dwarf clipped evergreens in the garden; sometimes they were scattered at random to create a pleasingly informal effect – bringing to mind a description in Lord Bacon's essay 'On Gardens' (1625) of the ground 'set with violets, strawberries and primroses . . . here and there, not in any order'. The rounded surfaces of feather-stuffed cushions powdered with slips also recall Bacon, in particular his 'little heaps in the nature of mole hills' set with periwinkle, pinks, cowslips and lilies of the valley, 'the like low flowers being withal sweet and sightly'.

Low-growing flowers were used to special effect in the rare surviving cushions which were made to support devotional books with embroidered bindings. Here, as on the sweet bags, the flowers were often raised in detached buttonhole stitch on grounds of silver gilt or deep violet or red satin. Also, 'very faire pillow beres' (pillow cases) were delicately embroidered with flowers in blackwork or in coloured silks and gold on white linen or cambric, their freshness complementing the fine sheets on the bed and in charming contrast to the richness of velvet and satin cushions and hangings. Slips and the coiling stems so popular on dress reappeared on these pillow covers, and were worked with equal refinement.

The coiling stem is one of the simplest and most ancient of patterns: it ornaments the borders in illuminated manuscripts, and it enfolds the saints in the magnificent vestments made by the medieval embroiderers. It appeals to the domestic embroiderer because it is exceptionally versatile, providing an easily drawn framework to fit any space, and made personal by the choice of flowers and the way they are worked. It can be used as a band or border, or as an all-over design – and often the two types of design were combined, so a border of honeysuckle would enclose interlacing stems of rose and vine. Its popularity in embroidery reflects the

Slips were perfect for the domestic embroiderer, as they were convenient and easy to work, either in the hand or in a small frame. How satisfying it must have been to see them mount up, and then to cut them out and move them about on the chosen ground until the right arrangement was found! Then they could be firmly applied with small stitches, these neatly hidden by a silk or silver gilt cord couched all round the edge. When new, the effect must have been brilliantly colourful; and even when faded to mere ghosts of their former beauty – like the primroses, pinks and marigolds on the darkened red and green cushions and hangings at Hardwick Hall – they retain their appeal to an extraordinary degree, still able to communicate the pleasure they once gave.

Seventeenth-century garden knot designs equally suitable for embroidery.

Book cushion, c1600, worked with borage, honeysuckle, cornflowers, roses, pansies and grapes on a coiling stem in tent and detached buttonhole stitch with spangles.

Early seventeenth-century pillow cover worked in black silk on linen.

Coiling stem border by Conrad Fyner (1481).

Stages in the making of a coiling-stem or waved-band design, from A. H. Christie's Pattern Design *(1929).*

sure, was their potential for needlework; but the 'pretty devices' these women made were now less likely to be worked in silks than in twisted 'crewel' wools on strong creamy twill. This material was ideal for wall- and bed-hangings and bedspreads, and it made an excellent background for exuberant floral patterns, reminiscent of blackwork, but now stitched on a far larger scale which made them look excitingly different. The designs included novel tulips and iris, and other flowers so exotic that they were not even to be found in the latest florilegia. Transformed into 'trees' with serpentine trunks and increasingly improbable flowers and leaves, these weird and wonderful plants soon became a feature in crewelwork. Two of the earliest examples can be seen on Mary Hulton's canvaswork cushion perched one on either side of an odd-looking 'rockery', and bearing pinks, marigolds and roses, together with altogether outlandish

delight expressed by Elizabethan writers and garden enthusiasts in the decorative training of roses, jasmine and honeysuckle over garden arbours – like the one described by Edmund Spenser in *The Faerie Queen*, evocative of a bed dressed with flower-embroidered hangings:

> And over him, Art striving to compare
> With Nature, did an Arber green dispred,
> Framed with wanton Yvie, flowering faire,
> Through which the fragrant Eglantine did spred
> His pricking arms, entrayld with roses red . . .

One of the pleasures of Elizabethan embroidery is to follow these flowery trails, letting them lead you back into the mysterious 'pleasaunces' of a lost garden world.

'LARGE BRANCHES FOR HANGINGS'

'Women', wrote Robert Burton, listing cures for melancholy in 1621, 'have curious needleworkes . . . and many pretty devices of their own making, to adorn their houses, cushions, carpets, chairs, stools . . .'. Equally therapeutic was the effect of working in a neat garden full of exotic, many-coloured flowers and plants 'which they are most ambitious to get, curious to preserve and keep, proud to possess, and much many times brag of'. The cultivation of these prized flowers was discussed at 'merry meetings' and so, we can be

(below left) *This crewelwork curtain (c1660) with its stylised oak leaves resembles the type of foliage pattern of 'large branches for Hangings' sent to India by the directors of the East India Company for the cotton painters and embroiderers to copy.*

(above) *Mary Hulton's early seventeenth-century cushion bears the arms of James I flanked by extraordinary multiflowering trees. The design of the pinks suggests Turkish influence.*

A multiflowering tree sketched from a seventeenth-century Indian embroidered hanging.

blooms whose appearance invites speculation. Where could Mary have seen anything like them so early in the century?

Rather similar trees clinging to rocky outcrops appeared in Mughal miniatures painted by artists who drew their inspiration from Persian models. But the Persian painters in their turn were strongly influenced by Chinese art, especially in the rendering of strangely beautiful rock formations. Mary could have seen examples of these, and of flowers unknown to the West like chrysanthemums and tree peonies, painted on one of the rare pieces of porcelain which reached England at the end of the long journey overland following the silk road, or perhaps on an early item of lacquer imported by the East India Company.

When the company was founded in 1600, the directors had fully expected to trade in Chinese wares – like most people in Europe at that time, they failed to distinguish between the arts of China and India – and their disappointment was considerable when they found nothing like them in the India of the Mughals. Eventually, in 1669, they struck on the idea of sending out from England some 'oriental'-looking foliage patterns for the Indian embroiderers·and cotton painters to copy. Though they have not survived, these 'large branches for Hangings' strongly resembled the multiflowering designs of crewelwork, and they were an instant success; but in copying them the Indian craftsmen – completely unfamiliar with many of the favourite English flowers and leaves – improvised 'after their own manner', and in the process turned them into just the sort of exotic creations the West expected from the Orient. The most desirable wall- and bed-hangings and bedspreads brilliantly painted and stitched with these entrancing make-believe hybrids were soon being imported in large numbers, and the bright colours, seductively curling leaves and spectacularly showy flowers soon attracted the attention of another

sisters' crewelwork bed an oriental-looking bird and exotic leaves inspired by Indian hangings are combined with typically English motifs such as strawberries and a running stag, creating a curious hybrid effect.

generation of embroiderers. Among them were the three maiden sisters of the Herrick family who, around 1705, embroidered a delightfully fresh and spirited set of bed-hangings now in the Bowes Museum at Barnard Castle. So obsessed and fascinated did they become in the undertaking that they took to drinking coffee at the expense of eating food, and according to the record worked themselves to death.

Major projects demanded energy and determination, and could take a long time to complete – although those who wanted to be instantly in fashion could always buy their hangings from a professional workshop. Early in the eighteenth century there was considerable competition for custom among professional embroiderers and pattern-drawers. The latter would provide the main outlines of the design marked out firmly on the material in black, and then it was up to the purchaser to choose colours and stitches to bring the pattern to life.

In the creative process it was easy to get carried away with enthusiasm, and this is evidently what happened in another splendidly idiosyncratic set of hangings made early in the eighteenth century and now in the Royal Museum of Scotland. Whoever worked them had obviously bought the linen drawn out with a typical Indian branched design, but to this she added a wealth of more homely flowers of her own devising – a subsidiary pattern of thin twisting stems curls round the trunks of the trees, bearing roses and other native favourites quite different in scale and character from those in the main design.

'CURIOUSER AND CURIOUSER'

'Curious' in the seventeenth century did not mean 'odd' or 'peculiar' so much as 'ingenious' and 'skilful', and as such it is the perfect word to describe the flowers which ornamented mirror frames, caskets and pictures in a type of raised embroidery now better known as stumpwork.

Flowers were only occasionally the main subject, but they appear in almost every piece – indispensable ingredients in the creation of an engagingly surreal setting for biblical or mythological stories, or encounters between characters representing the seasons, elements or continents. They were depicted with complete disregard to scale, often as large as or even larger than the people, lending the scenes a 'wonderland' quality reminiscent of Lewis Carroll's *Through the Looking Glass*, where Alice met roses, lilies and daisies that could talk, argue and change colour.

38

Early eighteenth-century crewelwork hanging in wools and some silk on linen, worked in long and short, chain and French knots. A typical design of serpentine trees with orientalised leaves, which has been enlivened with fanciful sunflowers, roses, hares, ducks and birds with redcurrants in their beaks. The hanging is part of a set, and may have been worked by a Scottish embroiderer with Jacobite connections, as a sunflower on one of the valances bears the cypher of James Francis Stuart, the Old Pretender.

A stumpwork box containing a bed of three-dimensional flowers.

A page of flowers sold by the London print-seller John Overton.

They were embroidered with truly remarkable inventiveness in a dazzling array of stitches by girls who, from the age of six, would have spent long hours perfecting their technique on samplers. This was the Golden Age of sampler-making, and however tedious the practice of stitches may have seemed, it meant that the girls would be capable of tackling the most complex methods with complete assurance when they began working on the inviting ivory-satin panels that would eventually be made up into mirror frames, caskets or boxes, or framed as pictures. The caskets were lavishly trimmed and fitted with trays and drawers, some of them concealing secret hiding-places. The drawer fronts were often embellished with stylised flowers in flat silk stitchery whose brilliance was only revealed when the doors were opened; and more delightful surprises were sometimes discovered when the lids of certain boxes were lifted and displayed a miniature garden or flower-bed, set in a removable tray.

Arbours of trelliswork, riotously entwined with multi-flowering plants, were another feature in stumpwork. Many of them were based on illustrations of biblical stories, though the artists who drew the patterns made them far more flowery than in the original engravings, and the embroiderers elaborated the inked designs still further, transforming the fruit, nuts, leaves and flowers into fantastic three-dimensional creations.

There was clearly a brisk business in supplying ready-drawn pictures and panels for caskets and frames. However, the embroidery was obviously extremely time-consuming,

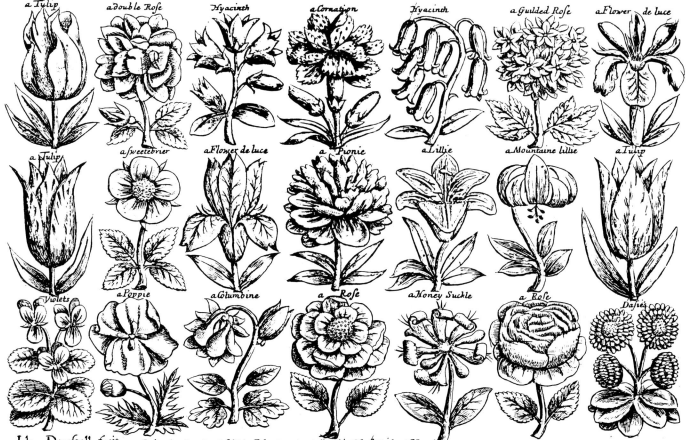

Unfinished stumpwork panel c1650 with scenes from the story of David and Bathsheba. The pool and trellis arbour are based on the engraving illustrated (right). The image has been reversed in copying, and flower and bird motifs included. The carnation is in long and short stitch in floss silk and resembles the motif on John Overton's sheet of flowers illustrated (opposite).

This engraving of Bathsheba bathing by Gerard de Jode (1585) was the pattern source of the unfinished panel illustrated.

*A silk and beadwork basket
made in the second half of the
seventeenth century.*

and probably for this reason several projects have survived which were never completed, or hardly even begun. The designs show a remarkable similarity of style, suggesting that they came from the same hand or workshop. Selling ready-to-work designs was a profitable side-line for the London print-sellers, who offered a variety of engravings and also sheets of mixed flowers, fruit and animals which the domestic embroiderer could adapt. The designs share a feeling of inconsequential gaiety, and the simple but lively motifs were all so appealing that it must have been difficult to know where to begin. Before attempting the people the embroiderer seems often to have started with the flowers, choosing the smallest and working them in long and short stitch directly on the satin. On her sampler she would have tried out many variations of detached buttonhole and needlelace stitches, and these were favourites for making individual petals and leaves. Some flower-heads were built up

by working the calyx and lower petals directly on the ground, and then applying separate petals, first worked in detached buttonhole stitch within a loop of wire wound round with silk. This method had been used in the sixteenth century – Mary Queen of Scots owned a coffer containing over seventy flowers 'maid of wyre coverit with silk of divers colouris' – but the seventeenth-century embroiderers elaborated on it, creating ever-more extravagantly frilled, curled and serrated petals and leaves that were shaded, striped and speckled to emulate and surpass the garden varieties.

Most extraordinary of all were flowers made entirely of purl – the finest imaginable wire tightly coiled into a narrow tube; this could then be curled round or couched down in lines, or cut into short lengths to make flexible beads. Purl flowers were inevitably more stylised than those in silk, and the method was often used for the more exotic-looking blooms resembling iris or pomegranates. The embroiderers also experimented with minute beads in shades of deep blue, amber, purple and green; these could be threaded on a length of waxed linen and couched down to fill the motifs, or they could be attached all over a firm ground to create a glinting mosaic of flowers – particularly rich on boxes or mirror frames. Strung on wire, the beads could be twisted into petal and leaf shapes to make free-standing plants.

Purl, silk and bead flowers also flourished on the embroidered bindings that were made almost exclusively for devotional books – the bible, the psalms, prayers and sermons – in the first half of the seventeenth century. Strangely these covers offer no clue as to what they enclose, (except for the few which depict scriptural scenes) and the enchanting flowers, birds and small creatures that ornament them seem far more appropriate to books such as Sir Hugh Platt's *Delights for Ladies* (1594) with its recipes for rose cordials and other flowery concoctions.

The embroidered books were designed for daily use; they were carefully kept in special bags, and when open were supported with a cushion made for the purpose, like the one illustrated on p35. They look fragile, but the raised cords and spangles used in their decoration prevented the reader's fingers from touching the areas of silk, and the covers were surprisingly durable.

Whether the embroidery was amateur or professional, the book was best put together in a bindery. The reverse of the work needed to be as smooth and free from knots as possible, as these would show through when the material was pasted to the boards. A linen backing helped strengthen and protect the upper material from the paste. Many of the books had wide silk ribbons attached through the front edges of the boards so they could be closed with two large bows, and a final touch of refinement was a bookmarker with tassels and cords complementing the colours of the binding.

Embroidered book bindings with stitch diagrams of the motifs: (a) Henshawe's Horae Successivae *(1632) with flowers and insects on an ivory-satin ground (b)* New Testament *(1625) with flowers and animals alternating on the spine (c)* The Daily Exercise of a Christian *1632 (d)* De Antiquitate Ecclesiae Britannicae *(1572) embroidered on green velvet for Archbishop Parker.*

a)

b)

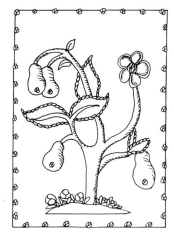

c)

d)

'LUXURIANCY AND PROFUSION'

'My Flowers grow up in several Parts of the Garden in the greatest Luxuriancy and Profusion' wrote Joseph Addison in a letter to *The Spectator* in 1712. His garden resembled 'a natural Wilderness', very different in character from the formality of parterres and display beds of tulips and carnations then in fashion. It must have struck many of his readers as odd and inappropriate, but such is the charm of novelty that this informal way of planting, imitating 'the natural Embroidery of the Meadows', soon caught on, and within a decade many gardeners had adopted – or at least adapted – the new style.

In embroidery a similar change was underway, and on furnishings of all kinds the customary neat slips and interlacing patterns were abandoned in favour of curving sprays, branches and garlands of flowers displayed in 'the greatest Luxuriancy and Profusion'. Exuberant poppies, hollyhocks, peonies and many others brought exciting shapes and seductive textures to rooms that were not only elegant, but invitingly comfortable as well; a riot of flowers on canvas spread over carpets and rugs in cross and tent stitch, in swirling all-over patterns often radiating from a central flower. Some designs were more formal, with central and corner medallions, or vases, baskets and cornucopias brimming over with loosely arranged flowers.

From the end of the seventeenth century till the 1760s flower designs were enormously popular on upholstered furniture, their treatment becoming ever more naturalistic.

Flowers with curling petals, leaves and stems were devised to harmonise with the scrolling ornament and serpentine backs of settees and chairs, matching in liveliness not only the line, but also the spirit of the Rococo.

One of the most spectacularly floriferous sets of seat furniture can be seen at Temple Newsam House near Leeds. It was made in 1745 for the picture gallery which was then hung with a green flock paper; against this background were placed chairs with tent-stitch covers depicting larger-than-life carnations and auriculas in their natural colours, with oriental poppies in vibrant blues on a Chinese yellow background: the arrangement must surely have created the effect of a brilliant garden border. The perfectly even stitchery suggests that the covers were made professionally; at the time this was easily arranged by the upholsterer or designer, though the cost might equal or exceed that of making the actual furniture.

Many embroiderers seem to have preferred to choose and work their own designs. At Arbury Hall in Warwickshire, Elizabeth Newdigate cleverly combined wild and garden flowers – pinks, honeysuckle and poppies in lavish armfuls on the dark green ground of a settee and eight chairs; and at Nunwick in Northumberland, Jane Allgood completed six seat covers and two screens in a magnificent set of rococo furniture which seem to epitomise Joseph Addison's 'Luxuriancy' in the choice and scale of the flowers. In a portrait of her at Nunwick, she displays a giant anemone and tulips worked in her favourite combination of long and short and tent stitch.

The Oriental poppy was discovered in Turkey in 1701 and is illustrated in C. Commelin's Plantae Rariores et Exoticae *(1706).*

Mrs Delany had a distinct preference for a 'very peculiar worsted chenille', and this she used for a 'group of scarlet poppies designed from Nature' on a glowing winter chair seat cover; it produced 'the effect of the finest painting, but with greater brilliancy and relief'. This cover was part of a set made for Delville, her delightful and highly personal home situated to the north of Dublin. Her diaries reflect the pleasure she took in making her own furnishings – 'She works even between the coolings of her tea' her husband Doctor Delany proudly reported. For the chapel seats chenille again seemed appropriate, with bright colours on a black ground, the design 'a border of oak branches and all sorts of roses (except yellow) which I work without any pattern just as they come into my head'. The dark ground had been chosen to give 'gravity', but such presumably was the luxuriance of the flowers that two months later she gave it up as 'too gay for the purpose'.

Always decisive herself, her comments on other people's needlework were sometimes caustic, as when she described a neighbour's effort as a regular '*fright* of a carpet', despite the fact that she herself had helped select the wools for it. Perhaps the pattern was too formal for her taste. In her own work she liked the spontaneous effect of flowers 'each different and evidently done at the moment from the original'.

It was this kind of naturalistic treatment that probably inspired the poet William Cowper's lines in *The Sofa* (1784) which describe a seat . . .

. . . of needlework sublime.
There might ye see the piony spread wide,
The full blown rose, the shepherd and his lass . . .

Lady Allgood showing off one of the covers (right) *for a set of chairs made in 1752 by William Greer. The tulips and anemones are worked in long and short stitch in wool and silk chenille on a deep gold tent-stitch ground; the designs and materials were probably bought on a visit to London.*

Design for the top of an eighteenth-century card table with 'fish' counters.

45

This sumptuous arrangement of poppies, roses, tulips, fritillaries and convolvulus epitomises the 'Luxuriancy and Profusion' of rococo embroidery. It was worked professionally in the brightest silks and metal threads on the white satin coverlet of a set of bed furnishings made for the wedding of Lady Louisa Carteret to the second Viscount Weymouth in 1733. The motif was repeated in the four corners of the coverlet with a matching but shallower vase in the centre (see cover illustration), and similar flowers including auriculas, jasmine and sunflowers embellished the valances, bolster and trio of cushions that made up the set. The latter were intended to be displayed pyramid-wise on the coverlet at the foot of the bed. (Reproduced by permission of the Marquess of Bath, Longleat House, Warminster, Wiltshire)

Cowper's peony and rose would very likely have formed part of a garland round a light-hearted Arcadian or domestic scene. This was a popular type of design, not only for seat furniture (see p98), but for screens, pictures and cushions as well. Even folding card-tables opened to reveal flower-framed surfaces on which lay needlework cards and counters, and purses spilling out coins to amuse or confuse the players.

Flowers on bed furnishings were in vogue throughout the eighteenth century. The earliest were splendidly formalised, but these soon gave way to more naturalistic and chinoiserie-inspired blooms worked in silks and crewel wools. Quilting was also in demand. In 1750 Mrs Delany was busy on a white linen coverlet 'worked with flowers the size of Nature, delineated with the finest silks in running stitch which is made in the same way as a pen etching on paper'. It sounds pretty rather than luxuriant, and this was to be the keynote later in the century.

In 1770 Sophie von La Roche admired bed-hangings of pale blue chintz at Lord Harcourt's with 'a border of the sweetest flower garlands embroidered in blue of the same colour'. These must have looked as light and pretty as those on the green silk bed-hangings of the domed state bed at Osterley Park in Middlesex, which Horace Walpole waspishly described as 'too theatric, and too much like a modern head-dress'. They were designed by Robert Adam, and in a later scheme for Lady Mary Hog of Newliston, West Lothian, he showed how well he understood the potential of needlework in interior decoration. Here the delicate effect was achieved in quite a different way, using tinted felt cut out in the shapes of baskets of auriculas and moss roses and applied to cream 'moreen', a ribbed woollen material with an attractive watered effect. Visitors to the Georgian House in Edinburgh can see how charming this kind of appliqué looks

on Lady Mary's bed: it is ornamented with a running pattern of applied flowers and leaves linked by ribbon bows, far quicker to work than time-consuming tent stitch.

To complete these elegant schemes there were silk pictures repeating the floral theme to hang on the wall. Posies and baskets of flowers were desirable subjects, and so were scenes from romantic novels or plays, like the enchanting oval silk picture shown overleaf.

Stitch diagram of a flower in crewelwork from Grace Christie's Embroidery and Tapestry Weaving *(1906).*

Delicate design for a bed curtain by Henrietta Cumming dated 1761.

Silk picture, c1790. The shepherdess with a bird may represent Leonora in Isaac Bickerstaffe's comedy The Padlock. *The garland of trailing ribbons and flowers – including passionflowers,* *geraniums and moss roses – is typical of the period. The faces, hands and sky were painted on the satin leaving the embroiderer to complete the stitchery, mainly in long and short stitch in silks.*

Ribbon-tied posies suitable for silk pictures by (left) *Maria Merian, and* (below) *L. Tessier.*

'SCOPE FOR FANCY, TASTE, EVEN GENIUS'
Elizabeth Stone *The Art of Needlework* (1840)

Mrs Stone is here describing Berlin woolwork which was all the rage when her book appeared. It had been introduced early in the century by an enterprising print-seller in Berlin, Ludwig Wilhelm Wittich, who had devised a new and distinctive kind of pattern. His wife, an accomplished needle-woman, enjoyed making her own small floral designs, and Herr Wittich had decided to try printing some of them on squared paper and offering them for sale. The so-called 'Berlin' patterns were hand-painted in brilliant colours (see illustration), each square of the canvas representing a tent or cross stitch, and the flowers – moss roses, auriculas, lilies-of-the-valley and convolvulus among them – were prettily arranged in wreaths, bouquets and borders.

By the 1820s special 'Zephyr' wools had made their appearance; they were quite different in texture from crewels, soft and extremely pleasant to use, and they came in a range of bright clear colours that were perfect for flower embroidery. Specialist shops sprang up offering a tantalising range of patterns; also of canvases in jute, wool, silk and cotton – far more varied than those of today – some of them coloured so the background did not have to be filled in; and of threads, ribbons and beads in profusion.

In 1851 Wilks' Warehouse in Regent Street was offering small squares for cushions depicting passionflowers, camellias, geraniums, pansies and gloxinias, and oblongs with cyclamen and poppies 'each surrounded with an elegant border'. There were also prie-dieu chair designs with lilies in 'Gothic tracery'. Berlin woolwork was well suited to elaborate seat furniture, and flowers proliferated

Berlin woolwork design of a basket of roses, pansies and convolvulus, hand-painted in brilliant colours.

Detail of Berlin woolwork c1840, with roses in bright 'Zephyr' wools and beads.

on settees, music stools and chairs of all kinds. Each chair had its own footstool, often worked with flowers and leaves in beads on a woollen ground. Lady Marion Alford recommended that the footstool should be as different as possible from the carpet, so that 'the poor thing may be spared the kick it invariably receives when the master of the house trips over its invisible presence'. This must have been a frequent occurrence in parlours where the floor was covered with a rug or carpet made of squares each stitched with a different flower design.

The exasperation of husbands whose wives were in the grip of Berlin fever is wittily expressed in a two-part poem printed in A. T. Morrall's *A History of Needlemaking* (1852). It begins with 'The Husband's Complaint':

I hate the name of German wool in all its colours bright;
Of chairs and stools and fancy work I hate the very sight . . .

His household is in complete disorder, and even on the rare occasions when he and his wife go out together:

At every worsted shop she sees Oh how she stares about
And there 'tis 'Oh! I must go in that pattern is so rare,
That group of flowers is just the thing I wanted for my chair . . .'

Undeterred by this outburst, his wife tells him she is about to embark on yet more flowers. She does not mention plushwork, but this at least would have introduced some variety, as the flowers were worked in high relief – the method involved working even loops over a gauge, then cutting and fluffing up the wool into a dense pile which could be sculpted into the shape of individual petals with scissors. Roses looked particularly impressive when treated this way.

Berlin woolwork began to take over the parlour early in Queen Victoria's reign, as this illustration in Osbert Lancaster's Homes Sweet Homes *(1929) shows. It was popular for men's slippers, braces, smoking caps and waistcoats as well as on furnishings like the banner screen and footstool seen here.*

51

'Parrot tulip' screen panel, worked in twisted silks in darning and stem stitches. This was one of the most popular patterns available from Morris and Co in the 1880s.

In the 1850s the character of the flower patterns changed: prettiness was exchanged for drama, with showy voluptuous and exotic flowers most in demand. These included arum lilies, cacti, daturas and fuchsias which looked particularly realistic when worked in wools brilliantly coloured with the new aniline dyes, Perkin's mauve and magenta. However, Lady Marion Alford found these colours 'offensive to the nerves of the eye', especially 'arsenical green', and their intensity was even greater when they were used on a black ground (see illustration on p81).

The gaudiest colours and most trivial Berlin designs appeared in the 1860s, when crude overblown blooms echoed the inflated curves of upholstery, and completed the floral takeover in 'Homes of Taste'.

'FRESH AS SPRING FLOWERS'
May Morris *Plain Handicrafts* (1892)

'What a rummage there used to be for anything tolerable', wrote William Morris describing his difficulties in furnishing Red House, his new home at Bexleyheath in 1860. He and his young wife Janey wanted it to be 'the beautifullest place on earth', and they quickly realised that they would have to make their own furnishings if they were to achieve their aim. Morris had already tried his hand at embroidery in 1855, when he was twenty-three, so when Janey brought home some indigo-dyed serge he was, as she relates: 'delighted with it, and set to work at once designing flowers – these he worked in bright colours in a simple rough way – the work went quickly and when finished we covered the walls of the bedroom at Red House to our great joy.'

The flowers were daisies, outlined in thick thread on the blue serge, and the charm of such simple embellishment – inspired by a Froissart manuscript illumination – can still be enjoyed at Kelmscott, near Lechlade, where the hangings are now displayed.

Morris's love of flowers is apparent in all his designs, and passages of his writing too, are particularly vivid – for example, when he describes his later home, Kelmscott, in springtime: the fields 'all buttercuppy', and the garden full of apple and cherry blossom, tulips, bluebells and 'heartseases'. In his designs he wanted to convey the excitement and pleasure that flowers evoked in him; but excitement alone is not enough to create good patterns, and it was Morris's *practical* understanding of the stitches and materials of embroidery that made his designs work so very well. Henry James visited him in 1869 and was impressed to see how 'he works it stitch by stitch with his own fingers aided by those of his wife and little girls' – Jenny and May, then aged eight and seven.

Embroidery was an integral part of everyday life in the Morris household, and there must have been much discussion of flowers, methods and materials amongst the family and their friends. In 1869 couching had been put aside in favour of an irregular darning stitch which was perfectly suited to convey the vibrant rhythms of plant growth that make Morris's embroideries instantly recognisable.

He designed cushions with motifs based on honeysuckle, roses and carnations, also portières and tablecloths, screen panels and bedspreads, all of which could be bought from Morris and Co. They were available either in kit form, where the design was traced onto silk or linen and a small section started to show the stitch, together with wools or silks for working; or ready-made, the embroidery completed by the professionals Morris employed – these were supervised by his wife, and her sister and his own daughters were amongst their number.

In 1885 May Morris took over the workroom at Morris and Co. An experienced and imaginative embroiderer, she had her own opinions concerning every aspect of technique and design: 'Unless embroidery is clear and bright as the day and fresh as spring flowers it is not worth looking at and not worth doing' she stated firmly, and her own work exemplifies her belief. A watercolour of her painted by Mary Sloane shows her working in the tapestry room at Kelmscott with no less than five vases of spring flowers round her. Like her father, she studied and drew flowers constantly, believing (as he did) that the designer's work should 'merely recall nature, not absolutely copy it'.

(above) *Book cover pattern from* Embroidery Work *c1912, a catalogue of designs available from Morris and Co.*

(right) *Book cover for William Morris's* Love is Enough *(1873), designed by May Morris in 1880. Like her father, she found inspiration in the coiling-stem designs of seventeenth-century crewelwork.*

An aesthetic interior entitled 'Greenery Yallery' from Homes Sweet Homes *by Osbert Lancaster. Note the embroidered portière, tablecloth and screen, and the sunflower in a vase.*

(a) Sunflower screen from Elizabeth Glaister's Needlework *(1880) (b) Sunflower and lily motifs from* Plant Form and Design *(1896), and (c) a tiger lily border from Miss Higgin's* Handbook of Embroidery *(1912).*

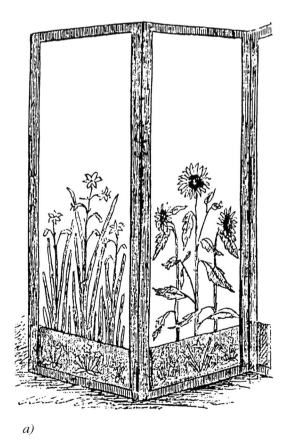

a)

b)

c)

By promoting good design, and insisting on the importance of beautiful materials, Morris and May transformed the look of nineteenth-century embroidery, and Morris's example started the craze for Art Needlework. However, the ladies who happily abandoned their Berlin charts in favour of patterns from the Royal School of Art Needlework or from Morris and Co, little realised how much more demanding the new style would be. The seductive flowing rhythms of darning stitch were by no means easy to execute – though this did not seem to deter the owners of would-be 'artistic' homes, who were thrilled by the new-looking flowers; and it was not long before 'many rooms were filled with pieces of linen, hung over the furniture in such quantity as to recall a washing day, each decorated with a spray of brightly coloured flowers'. The favourites were 'aesthetic' sunflowers and lilies, together with narcissus, pansies and wild roses, and these proliferated on curtains, screens, chair and sofa backs (known as antimacassars), and endless cloths and runners. In reaction to the gaudy Berlin colours, the flowers were now stitched in 'quaint and artistic' shades. Elizabeth Glaister called them dowdy, and certainly they looked sadly washed out in comparison to the glowing colours that were specially dyed for Morris and Co.

The quality of the patterns quickly degenerated, too, and soon 'startling sunflowers and staring ox-eye daises' became a cliché. It was Oscar Wilde's enthusiasm for the gaudy leonine beauty of the sunflower that had made it the hallmark of the aesthetic home. Like the lily, he found it a perfect model for design, 'the most naturally adapted for decorative art . . . giving the artist the most entire and perfect joy'.

In Mrs Newbery's work, the stems curve and then straighten into angular patterns in a way which is quite distinct from the sinuous line of Art Nouveau – of which, according to her daughter, she thoroughly disapproved. 'I like the opposition of straight lines to curved; of horizontal to vertical . . . I specially aim at beautifully shaped spaces and try to make them as important as the patterns.' She gave classes on 'Foliage in Outline' and 'The Study of Flowers in Nature', and constantly encouraged her students to devise patterns which, like her own, would create the most appearance with the least effort'.

Sweet pea cushion cover by Jessie Newbery.

'THE MOST APPEARANCE WITH THE LEAST EFFORT'
Jessie Newbery

A dramatic change in the appearance of flowers in embroidery came about at the turn of the century. In 1894 Jessie Newbery, a passionate advocate of good design and an experienced embroiderer with a deep interest in botany and gardening, started teaching needlework at the Glasgow School of Art. The increasingly sombre tones and trite patterns of Art Needlework were not at all to her taste, as she believed embroidery should be fresh and modern-looking; with this aim in mind she simplified the shapes of flowers, stems and leaves, gradually developing a highly individual style that was to be enormously influential. Her colours became equally distinctive, with pale clear pinks and greens, pearly grey and tints of mauve and violet predominating; and so did her methods, notably in her use of linen appliqué with the shapes clearly outlined in satin stitch, set off with some needleweaving, and often with inscriptions in bold, clear lettering immediately recognisable as hers. Though formalised, the flower and leaf shapes cut from coloured linen were always identifiable, and the stems were most skilfully arranged to emphasise the shapes of the cushions, curtains, table centres and screens they embellished.

Clover design for a table centre by Muriel Boyd Sandeman, a student of Jessie Newbery, c1912.

SUGGESTIONS FOR FURNISHING EMBROIDERY

Appliqué is one of the most effective methods for furnishings, yet it is seldom seen today. Indeed, a look through old periodicals and embroidery magazines shows a gradual decline in interest in furnishings from the 1940s on, with the exception of canvaswork, patchwork and quilting.

Embroidery has been slowly retreating into the picture frame and onto the wall, as a visit to any contemporary exhibition will show. Panels and pictures abound, but what has happened to coverlets, tablecloths and book covers? A coverlet will show off the textures of stitchery far better on the surface of a bed than hung on a wall, and, well designed, will do more for a room than any number of cushions.

Large-scale furnishings can be very satisfying to make, though the design and handling of large areas of material without previous experience can be daunting. 'You cannot begin by just throwing about sprays of natural flowers' warned Lewis F. Day when discussing appliqué in *Art in Needlework* in 1908. Whatever method is chosen, a disciplined approach is needed, and however much today's busy embroiderers may want to create 'the most appearance with the least effort' they must still make certain that the design underlying their stitchery is properly thought out for the object it decorates – if it is not, the appearance of the work will not come up to expectations, however much effort is expended on it.

Here it seems to me that the flowers in the florilegia and old pattern books have something unique and special to offer. Because they are so beautiful in themselves, they act as a spur to pattern-making, and positively invite you to work out pleasing arrangements as an excuse for using them.

Textural and colour contrasts in flowers are emphasised in Sara Norrish's 'Wintery Garden' (1990).

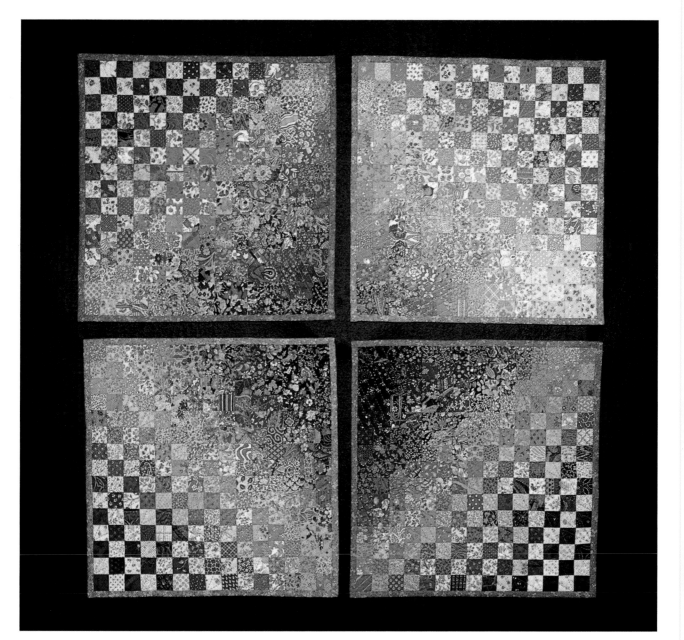

'The Four Seasons' by Deidre Amsden (1990). Patchwork in assorted cottons, machine-pieced and hand-quilted in a sunburst pattern across the checks, to create the impression of sunshine and shadow melting in a wash of flowers. The quilting lines across the dark areas represent rain.

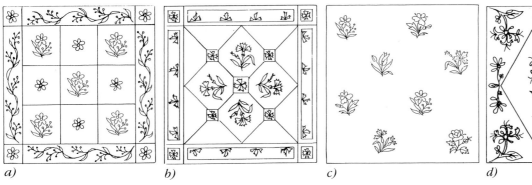

a) b) c) d)

Pattern-making using simple flower motifs. The square and diamond designs (a) and (b) were inspired by the eighteenth-century sprigs (c); the hexagon (d) within a square encloses a sixteenth-century honeysuckle slip illustrated on p33.

Rug worked in tent stitch by Sir Hardy Amies (1983–5) depicting his ten favourite flowers. The design was adapted from botanical illustrations by the Royal School of Needlework. The rich and lively effect is achieved by constant changes of tone in the wools.

The double hollyhock in Sir Hardy Amies' rug was taken from this engraving in A Garden of Flowers.

a)

b)

Rose designs showing radial and upright growth from Progressive Design for Students *by James Ward (1902).*

c)

One way to begin is to trace or photocopy and roughly cut out a number of motifs of varying size; place a sheet of tracing paper over 1in (2.5cm) graph paper, and then with a ruler mark out a grid of squares to enclose them. This may sound ridiculously simple, but in fact it demands practice and a discerning eye to adjust the scale and spacing of the motifs in order to achieve a well-balanced design; too small within the framework and they will appear 'unanchored' in their space, too big and they will overcrowd it and create a confused effect.

The advantage of this type of design is that it can be worked in a number of separate units; it is no more difficult or time-consuming than working a set of cushion covers, and no more difficult to handle. The rug pictured was worked by Sir Hardy Amies, best known as the royal couturier, but also an enthusiastic and talented gardener and embroiderer who has been stitching canvas designs for over fifty years; in its conception, he brought together ten of his favourite flowers, drawn from books such as *A Garden of Flowers* by Crispin de Passe and Thornton's *Temple of Flora*, and the result is a delightfully personal 'florilegium' made all the more decorative by the border that unifies and sets off the squares.

As much trouble should be taken with the border as with the main part of the design in terms of proportion. It can incorporate scaled-down elements or versions of the flowers, set in corner medallions perhaps, or on a waved line. The border and the grid itself can be made up of formalised stems and leaves. Flowers and geometric patterns make perfect partners in design, and from squares you can go on to diamonds, hexagons, circles and interlacing and knot patterns like those on p32-4.

If time is limited, it is quite feasible to make use of machine embroidery for furnishing projects. A bedspread I made was based on the square rose pattern (a and b) illustrated on p58, machined in outline with a perlé thread in the bobbin (cable stitch) which obligingly re-created the serrated look of the leaves. I planned a chequerboard effect, alternating the radial pattern with a single rose motif for the flat surface of the bed, finished with a plain surround edged with a band of leaves. I enlarged the motifs, and pinned stiff muslin over my photocopy which I held against the window and traced through. The muslin was tacked to linen squares and stretched in a hoop for machining, with the muslin uppermost so the outline could be followed swiftly. Using a strong matching thread in the needle and a tight top and loose bottom tension, the perlé wound in the bobbin produced an effect similar to eighteenth-century knotting – with the advantage that the thread did not have first to be knotted (using a special shuttle) and then couched down! I machined the squares together and emphasised the seams by oversewing them in satin stitch so they became a feature.

The third design (c) shows a rose in upright growth intended to be seen from a particular viewpoint, like those on Sir Hardy Amies' rug; whereas the radial designs look the same when seen from any direction. It is important to bear this difference in mind, especially when planning cushions, as the effect may be spoiled if they are tossed on their sides or heads.

Pamela Milburne's idiosyncratic version of Florentine stitch was inspired by the interweaving of flowers in her Kent garden, and creates a sophisticated, non-directional design. Her cushions evoke the harmonies and contrasts in colour typical of the plants she loves, and the staccato rhythms of the diagonal lines intrigue the eye.

The strong diagonal movement characterises Anne Kinniment's cushion, but here a gentler rhythm animates the willowherb, and the curving stems are skilfully extended to form a border round the central panel.

Cushion in Florentine stitch by Pamela Milburne (1980s).

Willowherb cushion by Anne Kinniment (1989). The calico ground is painted behind the flowers and quilted in the border.

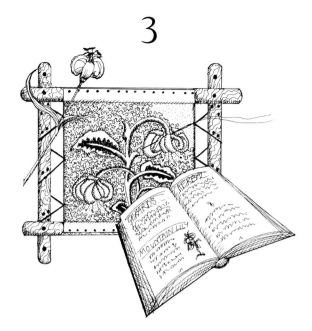

THE EMBROIDERER'S RECORD

'OUTLANDISH AND FANTASTICALL'

Over the centuries embroiderers have recorded the favourite flowers of their time, including amongst them novelties that were developed at home and 'outlandish' newcomers introduced from abroad. Some of their flowers were so formalised as to be unrecognisable, or so 'fantasticall' as to be obviously imaginary, and others were left out altogether. So the embroiderer's record can never rival in accuracy or completeness that of the botanical artist, or later, of the photographer. But what it can and does do is to provide a fascinating commentary on changing fashions in flowers which supplements the evidence of books, paintings and engravings, and offers intriguing clues as to how they were displayed both in flower arrangements and in gardens of the past.

Embroiderers chose, and still choose their flowers first and foremost because they like them. Some flowers immediately excite interest because their shapes, colours and textures are so suggestive of needlework – the distinctive markings on a fritillary, for example, invite exploration in bands or blocks of buttonhole or satin stitch; others are linked in the mind with people, places and events; and others have an irresistible quality, difficult to define, yet so endearing that we feel compelled to record them.

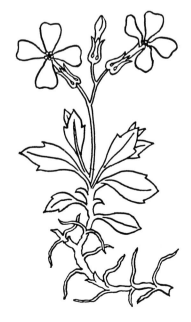

Pansy and aubretia by Grace Christie.

60

A stitch sampler worked by Grace Christie for an article entitled 'Flowers in Nature and in Art' in Needle and Thread (1914), illustrated with 'drawings from nature' which emphasise the individual character of the plant. Comparison of the horned pansy and aubretia drawings with the stitched versions show how she has simplified these further to make them effective as motifs. The pansy is in solid buttonhole worked from the centre outward, with each succeeding row taken over the heading of the last, and the streaks are in chain stitch; the aubretia (centre right) is in double back stitch with a stem outline and a white buttonhole wheel at the centre. The rose is in tailor's buttonhole, and the coral plant (bottom centre) in fishbone.

61

Portrait of John Parkinson in the Paradisus *holding a formalised rose campion (*Lychnis chalcedonica flore pleno*).*

(right) *The knots and flowers of Gerard and Parkinson's day inspired Jenny Chippindale's 'Box of Delights', 1990. The knot on the lid is worked with blackwork fillings in blue silk, and the sides depict the favourite borage, pansy, pink and peapod, worked as 'slips' in machine embroidery, cut out and applied to the tinted linen ground. The insects echo those of Elizabethan embroidery. The sweet bag is also machined using metallic threads, and the posy looks back to the three-dimensional creations of seventeenth-century stumpwork. The box shows a most inventive reworking of old motifs and methods.*

(below) *Columbine, pink, lily and pansy from* La Clef des Champs.

The response such flowers evoke reminds me of a phrase in John Parkinson's great flower book *Paradisi in Sole Paradisus Terrestris* (1629) – commonly known as the *Paradisus* – when he describes it as a 'speaking garden'; it is easy to imagine him in his own London garden in Long Acre carrying on endless conversations with his plants and encouraging them to flourish. And the embroiderer, carefully preparing her ground and selecting colours, threads and stitches to render the flowers to the best advantage, is similarly engaged in an intimate and affectionate dialogue. Her choice of flowers and their suitability as subjects for embroidery, is dictated by the plants she sees around her, and also by the patterns available, or the illustrations suitable for adapting for the particular piece of needlework.

In the past there were always some embroiderers who could draw out their own designs – and many do so today – but most made use of herbals, which described the uses of plants; of florilegia which illustrated their beauty; and of pattern books, intended not only for embroiderers, but for other craftsmen as well. One of the most delightful of these was *La Clef des Champs* of 1586, by the Huguenot artist Jacques Le Moyne de Morgues. He wanted it to be of value for needlework, and seldom can a book have provided more welcome inspiration. The flowers, birds and fruit have been simplified in outline, and need only the smallest adjustment for use as patterns.

The motifs on this red satin cushion include wild flowers, herbs and fruit; each one has been formalised to fit in the spaces of an interlacing pattern. Worked in metal threads and satin stitch in coloured silks, they have a jewelled quality.

It is interesting that Le Moyne called his little book *La Clef des Champs*, and not *La Clef des Jardins* – a hint that most of his subjects were field flowers which had been brought into the garden from woods and meadows – among them the eglantine and woodbine, pansies, primroses, cowslips, columbines and cornflowers. These were the great favourites of sixteenth- and seventeenth-century embroidery, as can be seen on a red satin cushion in the Victoria and Albert Museum; this vividly recalls the spellbinding lines in Edmund Spenser's *Shepherd's Calender* of 1579:

(right) Pincushion c1600, with flower sprigs including borage on a silver gilt ground.

> Bring hether the Pinke and purple Cullambine
> With Gelliflowres:
> Bring Coronations, and Sops in Wine,
> Worn of Paramoures.
> Strowe me the ground with Daffadowndillies,
> And Cowslips, and Kingcups and loved Lillies:
> The pretie Paunce
> And the Chevisaunce
> Shall match the fayre flowre Delice.

shown by the number of pansies (the pretie Paunce) and cowslips that appear among the pinks and lilies of needlework.

In this age, plants had been rediscovered as objects of extraordinary beauty and fascination, whereas before they had been appreciated principally for their medicinal, culinary and cosmetic properties. In his *Survey of London* of 1598 John Stow relates how the citizens went out on May Day to celebrate 'in the sweet meadowes and green woods, there to rejoyce their spirits with the beauty and savour of sweet flowers'; in fact he was describing a passionate enthusiasm experienced not only by connoisseurs like Lord Burghley with his grand gardens in the Strand and at Theobalds, but also by people who were new to gardening and who on their May Day outing might have eagerly gathered cowslips and wild strawberries and even dug them up for their own 'faire garden plots', then studied them as potential motifs for cushions or caps.

Lord Burghley's London garden was supervised by John Gerard, herbalist and the author of the famous *Herball or Generall Historie of Plantes* of 1597. In his own garden in Holborn, Gerard had collected together about a thousand plants and he delighted in describing the colours and textures of the flowers, often borrowing terms from textiles and needlework. However inaccurate he may have been as a botanist, his prose is a pleasure to read and full of interest for the embroiderer: for example, where he describes the 'glosse like velvet' on the 'Floramor' (*Amaranthus purpureus*) with its red and green leaves shaded like parrot feathers; or sunflowers 'the middle whereof is made of unshorn velvet, or some curious cloth wrought with the needle'.

Borage was particularly striking with 'its gallant blew flowers composed of five leaves apiece, out of the middle of like a brooch or pyramid'. This feature was repeatedly emphasised by sixteenth- and seventeenth-century embroiderers for whom borage was a special favourite: it was thought to 'make men and women glad and merry, driving away all sadnesse, dulnesse and melancholy', and was used in drinks, syrups and salads. It was also crystallised to decorate party dishes – as were many other needlework favourites like roses, marigolds and primroses; perhaps their colourful and decorative appearance, sparkling with frosted sugar, acted as further inspiration for embroidery.

Certainly brilliance of colour was bound to attract attention at a time when most flowers were small and fragile in appearance. For the embroiderer their jewelled look was an essential part of their charm, particularly as it could be accentuated by skilful use of silver gilt thread but basically it was the glowing yellow of daffodils and marigolds, the intense blue of columbines, and the wide range of strong reds in roses and carnations that made them so popular in embroidery.

The range of flowers in sixteenth- and early seventeenth-century needlework is surprisingly limited. Only occasionally did embroiderers include the Indian amaranthus and the nasturtium from Peru, and hollyhocks, crocus, cyclamen and love-in-the-mist were seldom, if ever, used. Yet thistles, perhaps because of their distinctive shape and emblematic associations (see Chapter 5), appear frequently. Gerard tells us that thistledown was used by unscrupulous upholsterers to stuff cushions and beds, and though Parkinson suggested them for a corner 'where something must needs be to fill up roome', they found no place in the new flower gardens of the day. Wild foxgloves too were excluded – but as usual the embroiderer went her own way, and foxgloves and thistles continued to flourish on canvas and in crewel- and stumpwork right through the seventeenth century.

pattern book by Peter Quentel (1527) (b) Thomas Trevelyon's Commonplace Book (1608) (c) slip for a cushion (c1600) (d) transfer pattern in The Embroidress *in the 1930s, and (e)* The Craftsman's Plant-Book *(1909).*

a)

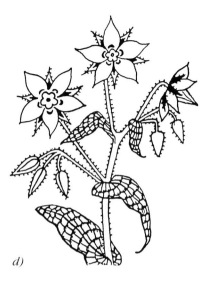

b)

c)

d)

e)

(left) *English and 'outlandish' flowers drawn with complete disregard to scale in John Parkinson's* Paradisus.

(right) *A lady of the Hampden family by an unknown artist, wearing a skirt embroidered with 'outlandish' lilies, crown imperial and iris. The formal patterns of the knot garden can be seen behind her.*

Parkinson was careful to make a distinction between the well-known English flowers such as pinks and columbines, and 'outlandish' strangers such as tulips and hyacinths from Turkey and sunflowers from the New World. These were to be treated like jewels, and not planted among the English flowers. Curiously this is not how they appear on the title page of the *Paradisus*, and gardeners and embroiderers alike tended to ignore his distinction and arranged their flowers to suit their fancy.

An arresting mixture of English and 'outlandish' flowers can be seen in the portrait of a lady of the Hampden family painted in 1615. English pinks, pansies and borage are worked on a twining stem of gold on her jacket, and they reappear on the skirt; but here they are joined by 'outlandish' lilies, iris and also the crown imperial, that 'delicatest and strangest' newcomer, a native of Persia which had reached England at the end of the sixteenth century. It was an object of wonder, given pride of place in real gardens and in embroidery, as on this dress where the lustre of gold, silks and pearls conjures up the magical garden in *The Wisdom of Doctor Dodypoll* (1600):

Where the light fairies danced upon the flowers
Hanging on every leaf an Orient pearl.

A crown imperial from the Florilegium *of Mathias Merian (1646).*

Pierre Vallet's etching of a martagon lily (below left) *emphasises the elegance of its re-curved petals; the orange lily* (Lilium bulbiferum) (below right), from Fuch's De Historia Stirpium *(1542), resembles the one in the portrait illustrated (p67).*

and this enhances its individual qualities, just as the inter-lacing patterns of box and clipped herbs in the knots of the real garden set off the prized individuals in the plantsman's collection. There are two lilies on the skirt, the upper one closely resembling the beautiful etching of *Lilium martagon* in Pierre Vallet's florilegium *Le Jardin du Roy très Chrestien Henry IV* (1608). Vallet was famous not only as a botanical artist and gardener, but also as embroiderer to Henry IV, and the flowers in his book – many of them rarities grown by John Gerard's friend Jean Robin in Paris – were intended as subjects for embroidery designed for the use of Henry IV's queen, Marie de Medici, a passionate flower lover and keen embroiderer.

Henry Hawkins might have had such a dress in mind when, in *Parthenia Sacra* (1633), he describes a garden rich in lilies, iris, pansies and pinks as 'the Pallace of Flora's pomps, where the wardrobe is of the richest mantles, powdered with starres of flowers, and all embroaded with flourie stones'. Using descriptive terms more usual in the world of textiles he brings the flowers to life: lilies of 'white satin streaked without and all embroadered within with gold' and a red one 'like a little purse of crimson satin'. For him, and for many of the plant enthusiasts of the day, the garden was as exciting as a theatre where 'delicious beauties stand as on a stage to be gazed on'.

The embroidery of the period succeeds in capturing the elusive 'star' quality of the flowers, and manages to convey the wonder expressed in the matchless prose of the period. It also suggests that the curiously sparse planting of knots and beds depicted in early garden books was a fact, and that the flowers really were set out singly with plenty of space round them. But perhaps most fascinating of all, it records the development of double flowers from the end of the six-teenth century on. In 1587, in his *Description of England*

A gardener setting out plants with plenty of space round them so that each is shown off to best advantage: woodcut from The Gardener's Labyrinth *by Thomas Hill (1577). The way the flowers are arranged in the flower beds closely resembles the cushion designs of the period.*

(first published in 1577), William Harrison noted 'how Art also helpeth Nature in daily doubling and enlarging the proportion of our flowers . . . for so curious and cunning are our gardeners . . . that they presume to do in manner what they list with Nature, and moderate her course in all things as if they were her superiors'. Both gardeners and em-broiderers wanted their flowers to be as showy as possible,

Double columbines from Sweert's Florilegium

double forms of primroses, poppies, columbines and roses, the embroiderers experimented with needlelace and detached buttonhole stitches to create ever more three-dimensional blooms, reaching their apogée in the amazing free-standing flowers of stumpwork.

Flowers that were curiously striped or marked such as tulips (see Chapter 7), or with voluptuous inflated shapes such as the mourning iris (*Iris susa*), proved irresistibly attractive in gardens and needlework – though embroiderers, just as much caught up in the enthusiasm for sports and strange forms, experienced none of the problems that beset gardeners in breeding and doubling new varieties. *Their* flowers could rival and outdo anything seen in real gardens, and they became more and more carried away in creating novelties unkown to botany, partly inspired by chinoiserie blooms seen on lacquer, porcelain and Indian-painted cotton hangings, and partly by the superb illustrations in the latest florilegia, to which they added their own 'fantasticall' variations. Embroiderers perusing the plates depicting the narcissus in Emanuel Sweert's ornate *Florilegium* of 1612, or L'Anglois' *Livre des Fleurs* of 1620 must have looked with delight tinged with incredulity at those with serrated trumpets and protruding stamens, either because they had already added these features to ordinary native 'daffadowndillies' to make them more decorative, or because it now seemed such a good idea to do so.

A needlelace flower on a long stem tops an ingenious revolving tape measure drawn by Sarah Siddall. In the original, the tape unwinds to reveal the following message: 'Take this small present at my hand who am your servant to command Mary Hanny 1687.'

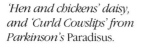

'Hen and chickens' daisy, and 'Curld Cowslips' from Parkinson's Paradisus.

*Mourning iris (*Iris susa*) by Robert Morison, 1680.*

(above) *A striped tulip, iris, lily and fritillary (right) add interest to this biblical tent stitch picture c1650, which depicts the three angels telling Abraham and Sarah that a son will be born to them. The bell-shaped flowers and pronounced patterns of fritillaries (especially* Fritillaria meleagris) *made them favourites in needlework, and these features were often exaggerated in stitchery.*

The title page of Emanuel Sweert's Florilegium *of 1612, depicting an angel filling the beds with flowers.*

Narciss. maior sive Pancratiui floribus Rubris.

(above) *Narcissus from L'Anglois'* Livre des Fleurs *(1620)* (left) *Pancratium from a page of narcissus in Sweert's* Florilegium.

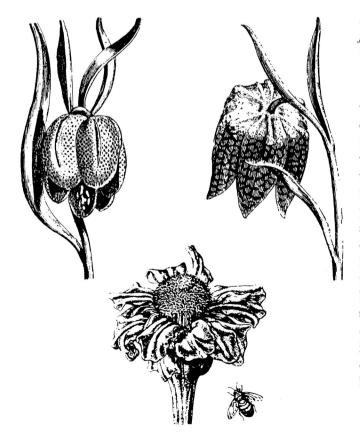

Gloves ornamented with flowers taken from A Garden of Flowers *by Crispin de Passe including the African marigold and two fritillaries.*

Then, when the *Hortus Floridus* of Crispin de Passe (1614) was translated as *A Garden of Flowers*, there were even more ornamental treatments to study and adapt. This beautiful book was illustrated with engravings of flowers depicted with attendant butterflies, bees and small creatures, and in which the skyline was exaggeratedly low. Looking at them today, it is easy to see how well they would work as patterns, yet despite many similarities between the engraved flowers and their counterparts in needlework, it is still difficult to pin down particular pieces of embroidery to the illustrations. However, one instance when an embroiderer undoubtedly used the book and followed every detail of the flowers can be seen in the pair of early seventeenth-century gloves illustrated above. Here the fritillaries, rose, tulip and marigold embroidered on the tabs of the gloves are copied directly from the book, and the shading of the engraving is reproduced exactly in the running and speckling stitches of blackwork.*

*As Vanda Foster has noted in the Costume Society Journal, 1980.

73

A gentleman admiring his hyacinths: illustration on the title page of Saint Simon's Des Jacinthes *(1768).*

(right) *The petticoat of Mrs Delany's court dress records many mid-eighteenth-century garden favourites, including newcomers like geraniums.*

Of the florists' flowers, the hyacinth was almost as popular as the auricula in eighteenth-century needlework, and this was an indication of the mid-century craze for them when doubles might change hands for as much as £200. Single hyacinths grew wild in Turkey and had long been cultivated in the gardens of Constantinople before they reached England in the mid-sixteenth century. In formal gardens they were displayed like tulips in special beds, but wild ones looked charming when grown informally – writing to William Shenstone in 1749, Lady Luxborough described them intermingled with cowslips and ragged robins in her shrubbery so that they resembled embroidery.

Mrs Delany recorded some double hyacinths in her 'paper mosaics', but for her court dress she chose a blue single, perhaps a special favourite as she rendered it complete with a broken leaf. Her passionate interest in botany made her keen to transcribe the flowers accurately, and the 'precision and truth unparalleled' that Horace Walpole admired in the cut paper flowers she made in the last decade of her life is already evident in the lifelike shading she perfected in long and short stitch in twisted silks. Such naturalistic treatment can be disastrous (as many writers on embroidery have pointed out), but Mrs Delany, as well as being a botanist, was also a skilled designer. She understood the decorative potential of the individual flowers, and was able to modify them where necessary and put them together in balanced and harmonious patterns.

The choice of flowers on her court dress is of particular interest, and anyone contemplating the re-creation of an eighteenth-century flower enthusiast's garden would find in it a ready-made plant list. All the florists' flowers are there, including five different anemones, striped tulips, and a polyanthus set beside an auricula. These two are depicted as plants

in the border edging the petticoat of the dress, together with a horned poppy and a pelargonium. This tender newcomer from South Africa was introduced in 1710; then known as *Geranium africanum*, it had quickly become a greenhouse favourite – its 'peculiar elegance' made it more striking than the perennial cranesbill, and more so even than the pretty *Geranium striatum*, otherwise called 'Queen Anne's Needlework' or the 'Embroidered Cranesbill', illustrated in Robert Furber's *The Flower Garden Display'd* of 1734.

Mrs Delany included sprigs from shrubs and trees like hawthorn, spirea and apple, and climbers like white and yellow jasmine and convolvulus. All these she could have picked in the enchanting garden she began making in 1744 when she arrived at Delville, north of Dublin, in Ireland. There were borders with double poppies, loosestrife and sweet peas, a 'Pearly Bower' wreathed with roses and honeysuckle, 'and wild walks' where cowslips, periwinkles and her favourite lily-of-the-valley flourished. Any new plant found on her botanising trips would be quickly looked up on her return. She found the *Herball* of 'old Gerard' useful for this, and with her eye for design she clearly appreciated the decorative qualities of the woodcuts. Many of her friends shared her interest in botany; for example the Duchess of Portland with her well-stocked garden at Bulstrode, who would gladly have provided her with any plants she did not grow herself and which she needed as models for needlework.

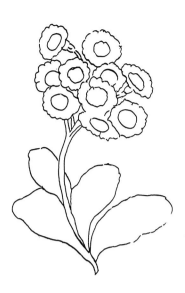

Mrs Delany's sketches of flowers for her court dress include a hyacinth with a broken leaf.

*Worsted hanging c1740
embroidered in wool in satin,
stem, long and short and
chain stitches.*

The title page of Robert Furber's
The Flower Garden Display'd
(1734), which depicts many of
the flowers embroidered on the
hanging illustrated.

The title page of Robert Furber's The Flower Garden Display'd *(1734), which depicts many of the flowers embroidered on the hanging illustrated.*

1 Yellow flowering Fig Marigold
2 Carolina Lychnoides
3 Dark red perennial Scabious
4 Everlasting Pea
5 Canterbury Bell
6 Sevile Orange
7 Murrey coulour'd Martagon.
8 Ultramarine Lark heel
9 Scarlet flowering Cotyledon
10 Purple single Virgins Bower
11 Sulpher coulour'd double African Marigold
12 Cluster Province Rose
13 Scarlet flowering virgins-Bower
14 Large Yellow Water Lylly
15 Spanish Marotto Pea
16 White Virginia Jasmine
17 Yellow Carolina Jasmine
18 Cobb Pink
19 Purple Shrub Fig Marigold
20 White flowring Martagon
21 Red Anthirinum
22 Large White Corn Marigold
23 Brampton Stock
24 Curl'd Leaf'd Bay in flowers

Few of Mrs Delany's contemporaries were as adventurous in their choice of flowers in their embroidery, though her friend Mrs Hamilton experimented most successfully in combining silk painting and surface stitchery – a technique which is now extremely popular again. Another exception is the unknown embroiderer who worked the worsted hanging illustrated. The design is a spectacular flower arrangement in a chinoiserie vase including roses, African marigolds, St John's Wort (*Hypericum*), and long stems of delphinium and hollyhocks which had been grown in sixteenth- and seventeenth-century gardens but were never taken up by the embroiderers of those days, perhaps because they were too tall to render as 'slips'. The convolvulus is *Convolvulus tricolor*, introduced from Spain in 1621 and a favourite in eighteenth-century embroidery because of its trailing habit. To the left of the vase are Brompton stocks, and a honeysuckle (*Lonicera periclimenum*) and pea entwine the tree trunk, neatly balanced on the right by a red runner bean and white jasmine.

The essence of the hanging is its delightful informality. It is as if the viewer had wandered into a glade in one of the newly fashionable rococo gardens, and indeed the extensive use of twining plants, the choice of flowers and their loose arrangement and colour scheme, all offer valuable clues as to how the coppices and shrubberies in many of the smaller mid-eighteenth-century gardens may have looked. Although in the great landscape gardens flowers had by this time been banished from the scene, there were still plenty of enthusiasts who were loath to give them up, especially when such exciting new varieties were becoming ever more readily available.

As much as being fashionable, flower gardening and the study of botany had also become serious pastimes, and new books on these subjects soon began to appear, with illustrations that were bound to interest the embroiderer. In 1734 the enterprising nurseryman Robert Furber brought out *The Flower Garden Display'd*, a lavish catalogue promoting the sale of plants from his Kensington nursery. The pictures had

These exercises in The Lady's Drawing Book *by A. Heckle (1755) would have been as useful for botanical drawing as for embroidery.*

(below) *'Geometric' garden and plan from* Rustic Adornment for Homes of Taste *by Shirley Hibberd (1856).*

a dual purpose, as they were 'very useful' both for garden en-thusiasts and 'for the Ladies as Patterns for Working'. This was followed by *The Lady's Drawing Book* with illustrations by A. Heckle which came out in two editions, one in 1755, and one in 1785 when it was described as 'an Extensive and curious collection of the most beautiful Flowers . . . the whole adapted for the Improvement of Ladies in Need-lework'. Both editions were attractively laid out as 'how to do it' manuals with exercises for beginners, taking them step by step from a schematised outline to a delicately shaded plant portrait. This format was ideal for embroiderers as it showed exactly how to formalise a plant to make it suitable for pattern-making, and the illustrations offered a treasury of ready-made motifs.

However, by the end of the eighteenth century there was far less incentive to adapt designs from botanical illustration because of the increasingly wide choice of pretty flower patterns delicately drawn out on silk and ready for working.

Then in the nineteenth century the majority of embroiderers became caught up in the craze for Berlinwork, the gaudy woolwork flowers which appeared in their homes echoing the blazing colours to be seen in the new 'geometric' layouts of the garden – Shirley Hibberd in his best-selling manual *Rustic Adornments for Homes of Taste* (1856) compared these to a firework display. The key word was 'dazzling', and it is fascinating that the most active years of the nineteenth-century florists – from 1820 to 1860 – exactly coincide with the Berlin craze; indeed the Berlin patterns capture the very essence of the florists' prize blooms as depicted in specialist publications like *The Florist* (1848–84).

Some of the most spectacular novelties were exotics culti-vated in the new greenhouses of the day. The passionflower (*Passiflora caerulea*) had been a favourite throughout the eighteenth century, but now it was joined by tender red and violet species, and other marvels like the velvety gloxinia and the wonderful royal waterlily, *Victoria regia*.

Chair back in Berlin woolwork c1850, worked with a waterlily and red passionflower whose brilliance is enhanced by the black ground.

(left) *Needlepainting in Berlin wools on a dark brown worsted ground worked by Lucy Trenchard, one of a series of floral pictures; they were so admired by Queen Victoria that a number were hung in Windsor Castle.*

(above) *Man's waistcoat, c1830. Narrow China ribbons were used like normal threads in the needle to form petals and leaves in a single stitch. Fuchsias were favourite subjects in ribbonwork, their stamens added in silk.*

Fuchsia motif from a nineteenth-century ribbon drawn by Joan Drew.

Newcomers amongst the florists' flowers were the Chinese chrysanthemum and the Mexican dahlia: in embroidery, some of the earliest examples of these flowers were depicted in a needlepainting by Lucy Trenchard (1775–1843). The flowers she chose suggests that it was worked in the 1830s when the dahlia (first seen in England at the end of the eighteenth century) was becoming 'the most fashionable flower in the country'. Lucy's dahlia is the pompom or honeycomb type which was the most popular of all, and with it she worked some of the latest chrysanthemums, including incurved and shaggy-petalled varieties. These had been bred from *Chrysanthemum indicum x chinensis*, the chrysanthemum held sacred in both China and Japan, known to the West through embroideries and porcelain imported since the seventeenth century but only appearing in English gardens in the 1790s. This was also when the first fuchsia, *Fuchsia magellanica*, was cultivated, soon to be followed in the 1820s by many other exciting species – for example *Fuchsia fulgens*, which can be seen in Lucy's arrangement, framed by the curving stem of a fruiting passionflower.

Fuchsias lent themselves particularly well to ribbon embroidery which was popular in the 1830s – many florists' fuchsias were then grown in pots and skilfully trained into eye-catching shapes. In *Old Fashioned Flowers* Sacheverell Sitwell makes the interesting comment that 'it was only when Fuchsia colours fell into disfavour, when purple or violet or magenta silks and reps were no longer worn that their skill in growing these standards or pyramids was allowed to lapse'. This was in the seventies when the strident, aniline-dyed colours of Berlin woolwork had given way to the subtler tones of Art Needlework, when the arum was replaced by the madonna lily, and refined rather than showy flowers came into fashion.

These swings of the pendulum can be followed in the changing shape of the heartsease (*Viola tricolor*): it had charmed embroiderers for over three centuries, and was then 'improved' by the nineteenth-century florists into a

round, fat-faced fancy pansy, with dark blotched cheeks in place of the whisker-fine lines that had once guided bees to its centre; later still it was slimmed down again to fit in with the native daisies and daffodils that embellished the furnishings in aesthetic homes. In 1855 however, when the Rev T. James deplored a Berlin pattern with 'pansies as big as peonies' and 'fuchsias as big as hand bells', his criticism might equally well have been levelled at the most exaggerated varieties bred by the florists.

Fuchsia study by A.E.V. Lilley from Studies in Plant Form and Design

In striking contrast, the flowers chosen for patterns in Art Needlework were most often based on meadow and woodland plants: primroses, speedwell, periwinkles, wild strawberries, eglantine and honeysuckle – the favourites of sixteenth-century embroidery, now in the 1870s back in vogue, and reflecting the latest garden craze for growing 'the dearest old-fashioned plants' in special 'Shakespeare' gardens modelled on those made in Queen Elizabeth's day, and planted with single rather than double flowers – cowslips, snowdrops and Herrick's 'smooth and silken columbine'.

At Kelmscott, William Morris re-created the impression of a 'flowery mede' and old-fashioned 'pleasance' embowered in the roses, jasmine and honeysuckle that animate his patterns. 'Be very shy of double flowers', he wrote in *Hopes and Fears for Art* (1882), and 'don't be swindled out of that wonder of beauty, a single snowdrop; there is no gain and plenty of loss in a double one'. In the 'Parrot tulip' screen on page 52 there is a background with a subsidiary design of snowdrops which appears to have been inspired by *Galanthus nivalis Scharlockii* introduced from West Persia earlier in the century – a cultivar remarkable for the long, ribbon-like spathe rising above the flower, faithfully reproduced in stem stitch in the embroidery.

Wild and cultivated pansies of 1830, from W. Cuthbertson's Pansies, Violas and Violets *(1898).*

Pansy motif on a man's waistcoat c1830 drawn by Joan Drew.

PATTERNS FROM PLANTS

A single snowdrop features amongst twenty-five English wild flowers which Gwen White has selected for their variety of form in *A World of Pattern* (1957). This page of flower designs is a good example of twentieth-century book illustration and might be useful if you are keen to make up your own patterns but are discouraged by the difficulty of getting your ideas on paper. Gwen White's flower shapes have been reduced to the simplest possible outlines; they have been 'formalised', so they already resemble embroidery motifs but are still recognisable as cornflowers, pansies and so on. Study the real flowers and the artist's outlines more closely to see which would work best in stitches and simple repeating patterns; this sort of observation will take you one step further along the way to making your own design. You will probably choose the shapes which are naturally flat, or can be flattened easily – the daisy and scabious, for example. Their centres could be worked in trellis stitch, which would re-create the tightly packed florets; or the whole design could be machined in whip stitch, in the scabious outlining each floret separately, and in the daisies allowing the lower thread to mount up in whirls by machining on the same spot.

'To the artist' wrote Richard Hatton in *The Craftsman's Plant-Book* (1909), 'a different treatment is as good as a different plant': Gwen White's page of designs could therefore provide the starting point for trying out innumerable stitch treatments and patterns – powdering for example, or with the motifs set in the spaces of a grid or knot as suggested in Chapter 2 p57. Then, the flowers might be considered from a different angle to see exactly how they are set on the stem, and how the buds, leaves, fruit and tendrils might be used in a slightly more complex design.

Miss Jekyll spoke of the importance of developing a good 'flower eye': 'If you are observant, which is one of the ways of being happy', she wrote in *Children and Gardens* (1908), 'you will want to know all you can about the wild flowers you see', and she went on to describe the parts of a flower, making botany sound not only interesting but fun, too. It is not essential to have a wide knowledge of botany to embroider flowers – a feeling for their beauty and character, and enjoyment in studying them closely is far more important – but some knowledge of the structure of a plant and the botanical names used to describe the parts of a flower can be helpful. Again, you must learn to be particularly observant so as to detect the 'hint of ornament' that makes one flower rather than another work in embroidery.

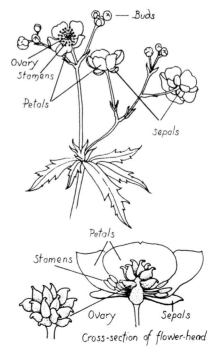

Mary Grierson's drawing of a meadow buttercup shows the decorative potential of stamens and sepals.

a)

In his study of love-in-a-mist (a) W. Midgley brings out the decorative quality of the leaves and stamens, and then shows how to emphasise and adapt this in embroidery in the design (b) for a border in appliqué illustrated in Studies in Plant Form and Design (1895). Compare his suggestion with C. F. A. Voysey's motif (c) from an article in Embroidery in 1934.

b)

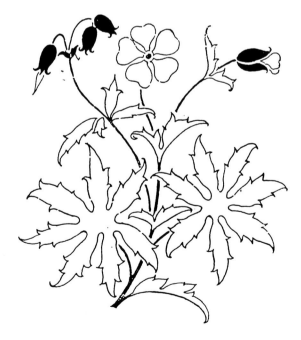

c)

The pattern potential in the cranesbill is brought out in Evelyn Dunbar's drawing (left) of the stems, stamens, fruit and calyx. Compare this treatment with C. F. A. Voysey's meadow cranesbill (above), fully formalised for use in embroidery from Embroidery (1934).

It may be the sepals that attract you – the little pointed 'ears' that appear between the petals when wild roses, potentillas and strawberry flowers, for example, are fully open. They are part of the calyx, the whorl of leaves that cover the flower when it is in the bud, and that are pushed back into separate sections as it opens. When the flower is viewed from the back they form a radial pattern as pretty as the stamens framed in the petals and provide a perfect balancing feature when *both* sides of the flower are worked – for example as in the cushion on p143.

The arrangement and colours of stamens, anthers and stigmas also invite the closest study. The harmonies of magenta, rose and violet in those of the fuchsia, the unlikely contrasts of acid green, indigo and puce in some cranesbills, and the variations of green in love-in-a-mist can suggest an entire colour scheme; and the varied groupings of stamens – long and short, straight and curled – create areas of 'richness and minuteness of detail' which can lift a piece of work out of the ordinary. The phrase is May Morris's, and her own embroidery shows the way with flowers and stamens glowing in the bright clear shades she loved – light turquoise-blue outlined with orange, and crimson laid against green.

Sometimes it is the sheer intensity of flower colour that is the attraction; Bernard Mitchell's place-mat, for example was inspired by the piercing blue of the dwarf gentian (*Gentiana*

The irises in Eve Dainty's picture (1989), were first painted on the silk ground and then built up in fragments of organza, the uppermost layer singed round the edge and caught under with tiny stitches. The petal markings were added in straight stitches and French knots. The contrast of swelling flowers and flat leaves was emphasised by painting the leaves on the ground.

Gentian place-mat in canvaswork by Bernard Mitchell, 1990. The plant-hunter Reginald Farrer described how the 'gentian literally burns in the alpine turf like an electric jewel' and this was the quality the maker wanted to convey.

acaulis), one of the many alpines that he grows in his Northamptonshire garden and uses as subjects for embroidery. His aim was to convey the precise colours and shapes of the flowers and their relationship to the leaves, and though he was not concerned with strict botanical accuracy, his intimate knowledge of his subject played an important part in the success of his design.

Look carefully at the flower stalk, too, not only to see how the flowers and leaves join the main stem, but to appreciate the stalk's relationship to the leaves and flowers. The colours of stalks and stems range from reds, blues and violets to browns and silvers, and they often harmonise with the flowers rather than the leaves – in *Rosa rubrifolia*, for

example, they are a deep reddish-violet which matches the sepals, buds and fruit, and is in contrast to the blue-green leaves. And if you turn these over, they reveal further subtleties of tone, green on one side of the central vein and red on the other, overlaid with a network of smaller veins in the complementary colour – an invitation to work them in open buttonhole over loosely laid satin stitch. The cineraria in the picture on p157 was chosen out of a whole boxful because the stems and leaves of this particular plant were as startlingly blue as the flowers, a striking effect seen also in sea holly, cranesbills and begonias.

Equally suggestive of colour schemes for needlework are flowers like the forget-me-not and the perennial wallflower, both of whose heads consist of florets in varying tones of pink and blue or mauve and yellow, so evocative that you cannot help but reach out for shaded or space-dyed threads. Moreover using the appropriate material can be as suggestive as the plant itself; for example, it was the discovery of a range of shimmering organzas that led to the making of Eve Dainty's 'Iris' picture: she saw the potential of organza to transcribe the ruffles and swirls of the petals as well as the rainbow colours from which the iris takes its name. And cobweb-fine machine embroidery threads seem purpose-made for describing stamens and the spiralling line of tendrils as they twirl round stems or reach out for a host's support. So often in embroidery these are used as no more than space fillers, and wriggle about aimlessly; but if you study the tendrils of growing sweet peas, bryony and passionflowers you will see how inspiringly different their tangled convolutions and tight, spring-like coils can be. The former remind me of pulled work and the latter of the lengths of purl used so extensively in the sixteenth and seventeenth centuries – though never for this purpose.

In *Nature and Ornament*, Lewis F. Day describes tendrils twisting friskily about, then gaily starting off again 'as it were on a fresh lease of life'. His words recall the verve of a tamboured chain stitch line (using a hook instead of a needle for greatly increased speed) in yellow silk on an eighteenth-century stomacher. Sometimes phrases suggestive of embroidery stick in the mind; they can inspire a project, and provoke as much excitement as might the sight of a real flower, or its embroidered counterpart old or new. Take this phrase from *Amiel's Journal* written one mid-November day in the late nineteenth century: 'Nothing could be lovelier than the last rose-buds or than the delicate gaufred edges of the strawberry leaves embroidered with hoar frost.' It suggests a hint of silver and iridescent thread and spangles, on an evening bag perhaps, the 'gaufred edges' of the leaves in needlelace and applied organza like the petals in the Hirst's picture on p119.

The early garden books are full of evocative phrases which bring alive the pleasure of working and being in a garden. In *The Country Housewife's Garden* of 1617, Paddy Killer came across William Lawson's advice to 'take the opportunity of a shower of rain' to grub out weeds. Inspired by his words, her embroidery conveys the country housewife's delight in every aspect of her garden, from the well-trimmed knots to the herbs and flowers that deck 'with sundrye colours the green mantle of the earth'.

Clematis Indica alia poliphylla, flore crispato.

Pr. Carolus Plumier Minimus Bolwaus a Regius deloneavit

(left) *The decorative treatment of tendrils in the passionflower,* Passiflora pedata *from C. Plumier's* Description des Plantes de l'Amérique *(1693) reveals a 'hint of ornament' that embroiderers might exploit in machine whip stitch* (above) *a sweet pea in crewelwork from* The Dictionary of Needlework *(1885).*

'A Woman in the Garden Weeding' by Paddy Killer, 1990. Machine quilting on a satin ground inspired by lines in the first garden book written specially for women.

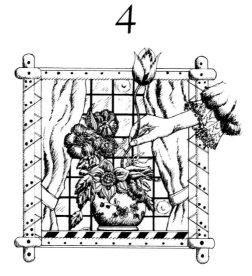

4

A GARDEN IN THE HOUSE

On his travels in England in 1560, the Dutchman Levinus Lemnius was particularly struck by the use of flowers to 'trimme up the house'. He was delighted by the sight and the smell of nosegays in every room, and in many homes the welcoming effect of 'a garden in the house' would have been increased further by the profusion of flowers embroidered on furnishings. Sprigs and slips were favourite motifs, as we have seen, but flowers in a vase were also extremely popular.

In the inventory dated 1561 listing Mary Queen of Scots' possessions, there was, for example, a set of bed-hangings ornamented with 'pottis of floures' in cloth of silver and gold. These were probably in appliqué, and similar in style to the red wool hangings also associated with Queen Mary which are decorated with vases of stylised flowers cut out of black silk and embroidered in yellow and blue (these are now in the Royal Museum of Scotland).

A flower-filled vase is one of the most versatile subjects for needlework, and designs for them appeared in the earliest pattern books. But embroiderers also drew inspiration from illustrations in flower books and from the real posies picked to 'beautifie and refresh the house', and their creations therefore echo the changing trends in flower arrangement, from the choice of flowers to the shape of vases.

The nosegays that Levinus Lemnius found so much to his taste were small bunches of mixed flowers; Parkinson called them 'tussie mussies', and recommended putting nasturtiums with gilliflowers. In William Lawson's *The Country Housewife's Garden* of 1617, half the lady's plot was given over to herbs and flowers for nosegays and garlands, among them violets, pansies, daisies and marigolds. The tiniest

Appliqué panel of a flower vase cut out in ochre velvet and edged in back stitch, French c1600.

(right) *Early seventeenth-century printer's device of a formalised arrangement which could easily be adapted for a box or cushion design.*

(top right) *Polly Hope's 'Dutch Flower Piece' (1977), a wall-hanging in quilting and appliqué, was inspired by seventeenth-century Dutch still-life paintings; it re-creates the lavish effect of a massed arrangement.*

nosegays were used to 'decke up the bosomes of the beautiful', worn pinned to the ruff or sleeve, or in the hair. The indignant moralist Philip Stubbes (1583) noted ladies wearing 'two or three nosegays in their breasts before, for which reason I cannot tell, except it be to allure their Paramours to catch at them'. If not snatched away by a gallant, the nosegays would have been put in a pot after being worn, as would the larger bunches decorating the house. Bulbous vases with curving handles were especially popular, for example, those on either side of Gerard's portrait in the 1633 edition of his *Herball*. The nosegays appear to have consisted of single examples of a number of different flowers, carefully set in the container to show each one to the best advantage.

This type of arrangement makes an ideal model for embroidery, as the individual shapes of the flowers stand out and can be treated in all sorts of interesting methods, from simple appliqué to complex fillings in blackwork and crewelwork. However, such a design risks a certain stiffness; some flower vases even had lids with holes for the individual flowers and although this ensured that they faced in the desired direction, it made for a rather rigid display.

In 1636 the Earl of Dorset (whose flower-embroidered dress is shown on p10) gave a great celebration at Knole for his son's wedding and ordered fresh bowls of flowers to be set in every window and fireplace. The vase of flowers in crewelwork pictured containing a rose, pansy, pink, borage and tulips, gives an idea of how these arrangements might have looked.

London Printed by
Adam Islip Joice Norton
and Richard Whitakers
Anno 1633.

(above) *Ornate vase with a lid for holding flowers in place, from G. B. Ferrari's* De Florum Cultura Libri IV *(1633).*

(above left) *Stylised roses in a vase form the centre of a design for needle-made lace of late sixteenth-century Italian origin.*

(above) *An arrangement from John Rea's* Flora *(1676). The shapes of the flowers stand out against the dark ground, suggesting a treatment in Assisi work.*

(left) *A mixed bouquet of native and exotic flowers features on each side of John Gerard's portrait in the 1633 edition of his* Herball. *Each vase is framed to fine effect by an arch and set off by a distant view; the one on the left is topped with bananas, newly imported from India.*

(left) *Detail of a crewelwork hanging c1650: a nicely balanced posy including flamed tulips, borage and heartsease, clearly recognisable in contrast to the 'outlandish' creations in the corners.*

Vase design from Thomas Trevelyon's Chronicle *(1616).*

Vases containing a single type of flower – roses or pinks, for example – were also popular, and there were attractive formalised designs for these among Thomas Trevelyon's patterns. Potted-up flowers were taken indoors when none were available in winter; arrangements with artificial flowers in silk and embroidery would sometimes take their place. We can imagine how these might have looked from a description of a winter wedding celebrated with a 'Masque of Flowers' in the Banqueting House in Whitehall in 1633: an entire garden, complete with an arbour and knots ornamented with great 'Pottes of Jilliflowers', made a fantastic setting for masquers wearing white satin doublets 'imbroidered and cut into lilies-flowers'.

PYRAMIDS AND BASKETS

A further fascinating example of embroidery supplementing our knowledge of changing flower fashions is to be found in the designs for early eighteenth-century chair-seat covers, where large Delft vases with special spouts for holding individual flowers are depicted. Queen Mary II set the vogue for these blue and white vases when she ordered some from Holland; these can still be seen at Hampton Court. The idea was similar to that of the containers illustrated by Ferrari (see p93), but the Delft versions often resembled a pyramid in shape, or occasionally a pagoda, with tiers or separate sections graduated in size and fitting one on top of the other. These were massive vases, sometimes standing head high, and were originally thought to have been designed for tulips; however, the embroidered versions at Croft Castle, Herefordshire and Doddington Hall, Lincoln show clearly that they were filled with a variety of carnations, lilies, peonies and other flowers. Any stiffness in design was re-

lieved by the stunning contrast of blue and white in the distinctively shaped pots, and the bright reds, greens and yellows of the flowers and leaves. The fashion never caught on in Holland, though mixed bouquets in more conventionally shaped Delft vases and in jugs, ewers and glass goblets were depicted in countless Dutch flower paintings.

One particularly talented artist and intrepid entomologist was Maria Sybilla Merian (1647–1717); she also followed in these traditions, having worked with one of the foremost flower painters, Abraham Mignon. In her *Neues Blumenbuch* of 1680, a highly decorative florilegium, she has depicted a beautiful basket and vase of flowers, and in her preface she makes it clear that the engravings in her book were intended as patterns for needlework. Some of the prettiest plates illustrate the loosely tied nosegays with twining ribbons which were to become such favourites in the eighteenth century.

'Tulip' vase filled with mixed flowers embroidered on a chair at Croft Castle.

A basket and a chinoiserie vase from Maria Merian's Neues Blumenbuch *(1680). Note how the shape and pattern of the containers enhance the loose arrangement of the flowers.*

1 Perennian dwarf Sunflow. 8 Pansies or Harts-ease. 17 Fraxinella. 26 White Jasmine.
Ultramarine & Prussian. 9 Maidens blush Rose. 18 Moß province Rose. 27 Scarlet Geranium.
2 New Iris Major. 10 Yellow Jasmine. 19 Double Virginian silk Graß. 28 Yellow Martegon.
Blew Nigella or 11 Blew Corn flower. 20 White Rose. 29 Red Martegon.
3 Fennel flower. 12 Blush Belgick Rose. 21 Dutch hundred leav'd Rose 30 Teucrium or Germander.
4 Moon Trefoile. 13 The Francford Rose. 22 White Batchellers Buttons 31 Mountain dwarf Pink.
5 Upright Sweet William. 14 Double Martagan. 23 Rosa Munde. 32 Yellow icon Marygold.
6 Saxifrage. 15 Orchis or Bee flower. 24 Mountain Lychnis. 33 Purple sweet Pea.
7 Cinque foile. 16 Scarlet Colutea. 25 Dwarf Iris strip'd. 34 Greek Valerian.

JUNE

Printed for John Bowles at the Black Horse in Cornhill

The June page from Robert Furber's Twelve Months of Flowers, *1730. In the 1734 version,* The Flower Garden Display'd, *the arrangements were recommended as embroidery patterns.*

Anne Grant's wall-hanging in silk and wool on canvas is signed and dated 1750. The dramatic build-up of patterns in the tile perspective and framing arches makes a most decorative setting for the carefully grouped vases, pots and baskets.

The gorgeous flower arrangements in Robert Furber's *The Flower Garden Display'd* (1734) were engraved from paintings by the Flemish artist Pieter Casteels; these included all sorts of vases which the embroiderer could adapt. As is so often the case in Dutch paintings, the flowers were chosen to create the maximum decorative effect, irrespective of whether they flowered at the same season, and masses of different blooms were skilfully arranged to give a seemingly natural, but in fact most artificially contrived impression. In embroidery, the stiffness of earlier designs was replaced by exaggeratedly curving stems and leaves, with flowers shaded to give a three-dimensional appearance. Some simplification was essential when illustrations such as Casteels' were used as patterns, and this often makes it difficult to trace the embroidered versions to a particular engraved source.

Flower-filled vases were also a speciality of the pattern-drawers, and the spontaneity of some eighteenth-century designs suggests that they were inspired by real flowers arranged at home. This is certainly true of the hanging which depicts five vases of mixed flowers embroidered in 1750 by Anne Grant of Monymusk. It must surely have been for some celebration that the columns of the arcade on the terrace were entwined with honeysuckle and the arches decked with lavish festoons. The largest arrangement could have been inspired by Furber, but the two small vases on either side of the elegant potted tree, and also the pair of oriental vases, have been filled much more freely with roses, peonies and what might be an early embroidered version of gladiolus. If Anne Grant did devise the design herself she must have made sketches of the flowers at the time, as the hanging is worked very finely in tent stitch and would have taken a considerable time to complete.

Detail of a settee cover in tent stitch, based on William Kent's illustration to Gay's Fables. *The garland of mixed flowers is typical of eighteenth-century furniture designs, and the vase in the fireplace reflects the contemporary fashion for arrangements in chinoiserie containers.*

'The Painter who pleased Nobody and Everybody' by William Kent, which was adapted for the settee design on this page.

A gardener offers a bouquet to a lady: the frontispiece to The Complete Florist (1775).

Flower-filled vases were popular subjects for eighteenth-century tent-stitch furnishings, and in particular for screens and seats of all kinds. It was the fashion to place large flower arrangements in the fireplace during the summer months, and an interesting example of this can be seen in the settee cover on p98. The design was based on William Kent's illustration to 'The Painter who pleased Nobody and Every-body' in John Gay's *Fables* (1738). In the engraving the fireplace is empty, and clearly the vase was introduced by the pattern-drawer to make the rather bleak studio look more inviting and decorative. In *The City Gardener* (1722), Thomas Fairchild described the custom of town dwellers to furnish their rooms 'with Basons of Flowers and Bough Pots, rather than not have something of a garden before them' and the embroidery shows how effective these 'bough pots' could look.

The professional embroiderers also worked flower arrangements in silks and gold to create the most opulent effect on bed furnishings – for example, the coverlet on p46 and on dresses such as the extraordinary outfit worn by Lady Huntingdon and described by Mrs Delany in her wittiest and most waspish vein:

Her petticoat was black velvet embroidered with chenille, the pattern *a large stone vase* filled with *ramping flowers* that spread over a breadth of the petticoat from the bottom to the top; between each vase of flowers was a pattern of gold shells, and foliage embossed and most heavily rich; the gown

was white satin embroidered also with chenille mixt with gold ornaments, *no vases* on the *sleeve*, but *two or three on the tail*; it was a most laboured piece of finery, the pattern much properer for a stucco staircase than the apparel of a lady – a mere shadow that tottered under every step she took under the load.

One of the most accomplished yet least known embroiders of the eighteenth century was Miss Anne Morritt of Rokeby Park in Co Durham. As early as 1738, when she was twelve, she worked a ribbon-tied bouquet of moss roses and honeysuckle in coloured silks; but she was soon to develop a far more assured and personal style as the first exponent of 'needlepainting', using crewel wools to recreate the effect of a painting. An impressive series of her woolwork pictures (among them the flower piece illustrated on p100), and her portrait by Benjamin West showing her engaged in her embroidery, are preserved at Rokeby. Her stitching is remarkable for its spontaneity; its style is freer and less laboured than the attempts made by the more celebrated Mrs Knowles and Miss Linwood to copy every brushstroke of the well-known oil paintings they reproduced in wool.

Many of Miss Morritt's pictures have been traced to their source, but the flower piece remains elusive; she may well have stitched it from life or from a rapid sketch, as she did in the superb portrait of the family's old gardener holding two pretty baskets, one of fruit and one of flowers, which can also be seen in the house.

Needlepainting of an arrangement including double or 'plush' anemones, bunch-flowered narcissus (Narcissus tazetta) and a hyacinth, worked by Anne Morritt in worsted wools on twill entirely in straight stitches. Miss Morritt developed this technique and used it with complete assurance, giving her stitchery a bravura quality.

Many of the special containers for flowers were made in silver, pottery and porcelain and were also recorded in needlework, but some of the simplest and yet most decorative were baskets. A charming example of the popular oval shape can be seen in the detail from the six-panel screen worked by Lady Julia Calverley in 1727, at Wallington in Northumberland (see p1). In it, a boy is apparently about to offer a basket of flowers to a lady out walking with her pet squirrel on her wrist. Baskets of parrot tulips, moss roses, convolvulus and liles-of-the-valley worked on white satin were favourite subjects for pole screens and pictures in late Georgian and Regency homes, and they also appeared as motifs on printed cottons, making useful centrepieces for patchwork quilts. 'Have you remembered to collect pieces for the patchwork?' wrote Jane Austen to her sister Cassandra in 1811; and she went on with a touch of exasperation 'we are now at a standstill'. The quilt they worked can still be seen at Chawton in Hampshire, pieced together from small diamond-shaped panels cut from flowered, striped and sprigged fabrics with a larger central panel depicting a flower-filled basket.

FLORAL ORNAMENTS

Baskets with exaggeratedly curved handles and elaborately ornamented vases were among the best-selling patterns of the Berlin designers, and magazines like *Godey's Lady's Book* were full of suggestions for novel arrangements for 'enlivening the aspect of an apartment'. The writers' advice on how to create the maximum impact was to use the most startling colour contrasts possible, and might have been written with the Berlin enthusiast in mind; and when

Eighteenth-century design for alternative garlands and baskets of flowers.

(below) *The chapter heading for 'Floral Ornaments' in Shirley Hibberd's* Rustic Adornment for Homes of Taste *shows a flower-filled basket similar to those in the Berlin designs.*

101

describing, in *Window Gardening* (1874), how his readers should choose an appropriate setting for their creations, Frank Burbidge found the perfect analogy in Berlin wool-work: 'In arranging flowers it is well to bear in mind the laws of worsted work, and when we desire to adorn our rooms with flowers we should consider the grounding to be prepared for them, as if it were a cushion.' The incredible elaboration of Victorian arrangements made a plain background highly desirable; though in many over-decorated 'Homes of Taste' such a setting must have been hard to find.

Some of the most ornate displays were seen on dining tables; indeed, the ideas in *Floral Designs for the Table* written by John Perkins in 1877 for garlanding and swagging cloths with real leaves and flowers could equally well have served as embroidery patterns. Mrs Haweis, one of the most voluble commentators of Victorian fashion, found 'flowers on the table nearly as necessary as food . . . They create a spark in the most inane . . . You can't talk about the plate and glass, but you can always remark upon the flowers; and if you are too miserable to speak, you can at least look at the combinations and reflect how much better ones you have seen.'

Mrs Haweis' advice could equally well have applied to the three-dimensional arrangements in woolwork set under large glass domes to protect them from dust. Instructions for making these flowers were to be found in magazines, and also in Caulfield and Saward's *Dictionary of Needlework* (1883); flamboyant orchids were a popular choice, and so were camellias, roses, hyacinths and geraniums. The flowers were built up on bent wire shapes worked over with wool

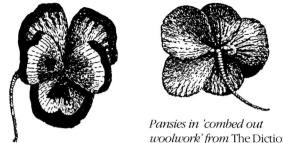

Pansies in 'combed out woolwork' from The Dictionary of Needlework.

'so that they stand erect'. The *Dictionary* also explained how to make beaded and 'Detached Flowers' which, like those in wool, could be made with long stems or short ones suitable for using as a small border round a circular mat for a carafe or claret jug. The 'Detached Flowers' were made from combed and fluffed-out Berlin wool glued down on velvet; these were sometimes set on imitation 'moss' which was made by knitting up a length of wool in shades of green, and then dampening, ironing and finally unravelling it and couching it down in small loops.

How refreshingly simple William Morris's 'Flower Pot', designed in about 1880, must have seemed in comparison to these contrived displays! Here was a perfectly balanced design 'distinctly apart from the old nosegay masses and the modern jumble' as described by William Robinson in *The English Flower Garden* (1883). Robinson wanted flower arrangements to 'seek unity, harmony and simplicity of effect, rather than complexities, many of which would involve much wearisome labour' – advice which is equally applicable to embroiderers then and now.

'The Flower Pot' cushion designed by William Morris c1880, and worked by May Morris.

'A FLOWERLESS ROOM IS A SOULLESS ROOM'
Vita Sackville-West

Flowers in a vase provide endless inspiration for embroidery. For the beginner as much as for the experienced embroiderer, there is much to be learnt and enjoyed in the sequence of picking a posy, choosing a vase, and finding the right place for it in the house. Putting one flower with another to make up a small tussie mussie is like building up a design. You may have a definite purpose in mind – a posy for the bedroom of a friend coming to stay for example, in which case you might choose colours and flowers you know will be appreciated; or perhaps the flowers are gathered on impulse because the markings, depth of colour and frilled petals of, say, a pink, attract the attention so strongly that you stoop to pick it; and then choose others to go with it, more pinks perhaps, or a viola or two of equal intensity but quite different shape, and a sprig of purple sage to add its soft texture to the posy. You can compose the tussie mussie as you walk from one plant to the next, stripping off unwanted leaves and cutting the stems to a particular length as you go along so that you have a tight bunch to put straight in a vase as a ready-made arrangement. Or you can gather them loosely and let the choice of vase determine the stalk length and how many leaves should be discarded.

Many would share Vita Sackville West's belief that 'a flowerless room is a soulless room', which 'even one solitary little vase of living flowers may redeem'. It may be that, sub-consciously, I always pick flowers with embroidery in mind; many times I have put a vase down on the round green table by the kitchen window and found its appearance so delightful that my one idea has been to record it in needlework.

Beverley Nichols put this idea very neatly when he said 'every flower arrangement is a form of self expression'; and it is also a most pleasurable way of developing good judgement in colour, shape and texture. Choosing the right vase can be just as instructive, and a great deal can be learnt about the principles of design simply by setting a posy in a number of differently shaped vases, and seeing which suits it best. Balance, scale and rhythm will all play their part in your decision. Of these, balance is the most crucial: a top-heavy or lop-sided arrangement will look as worrying in embroidery as it does in the home.

Some vases have shapes which make them particularly useful as models for needlework. Those with high necks and small openings support the stems, and often result in the flowers arranging themselves; in particular, they prevent overcrowding, which is as much a pitfall in needlework as in real arrangements.

'To show off to the best advantage, flowers should have nodding room' wrote Julia Berrall in her *History of Flower Arrangement* (1953); not only does this draw attention to their individual forms but – and this is especially important in needlework designs – the space between the stems assumes more interesting shapes.

(above) *A 'Flower Circle' based on a spring posy picked with pattern-making in mind.*

A vase of well-spaced flowers 'for white or coloured work' from Joan Drew's Embroidery and Design.

Try it out. If you have no garden, a bunch of five anemones makes a perfect starting point – there are no leaves to distract you, but instead each stem sports a frilly ruff of green fronds, sometimes immediately below the flower, sometimes lower down the stem. Moreover, anemone stems often curve attractively, so if the shapes do not look quite right when you first place the flowers in the vase, simply move a couple of stems just below the ruff, and the appearance of the ensemble will be altered. Or look at the vase from below, or from above, as a different viewpoint will transform the effect again. Once the flowers and vase are in harmony, make a rough outline sketch, or paint the shapes of the flowers and vase directly onto your material. This does not have to be done accurately, indeed, paint bleeding out beyond the outlines can add to the decorative effect. A simple alternative would be to cut out the shapes of the flowers and apply them separately.

A mixed bunch will probably include bright red, purple and magenta; these shades in particular are intensified by the complementary green of the ruff and the striking indigo and violet of the central boss and stamens. Some anemones, white ones in particular, have bright acid-green stamens, and stems overlaid with violet or deep pink. The colours are so exciting that they invite immediate comparison with threads, and the threads you have available may well determine the method you choose. My favourite winter pick-me-up, when the flowers in the garden have dwindled away, is to buy such a bunch in order to embroider it. I often outline the flowers in machine whip stitch on a painted ground, but each bunch offers a new range of possibilities in terms of vase, background and treatment.

Anemone from J. Foord's Decorative Plant Studies *(1909), showing the arrangement of stamens round the dome-shaped stigma.*

A vase of anemones interpreted by Val Tulloch in two different ways: applied in felt on a blackwork-ornamented ground of cream and beige even-weave curtain fabric and in coloured silks outlined in couching on a ground of pattern-couched gold.

(above right) *'Anemones' by the author (1985). Hand and machine embroidery on painted crêpe de chine. The stems of the anemones are in silk-covered wire, and the ruffs in whip stitch. The picture records a favourite watercolour and the author's embroidery journal, open at May, when an exhibition of her work took place.*

'We've been having lectures on flower arrangement at the Women's Institute', says Rowena, a character in Barbara Pym's novel *A Glass of Blessings* (1958). 'I discovered I'd been doing mine wrong for years. My arrangements which I thought so pretty had no interesting focal point!' Doubtless Rowena had been putting her flowers simply in small vases with a few sprigs of foliage to support them. It is a method that has never been out of fashion, whatever the pundits may say. As a basis for embroidery design it would need tightening up.

Here the example of paintings can be instructive. Both Raoul Dufy and Charles Rennie Mackintosh were superb textile artists as well as painters, and their sense of design makes their treatment of flowers particularly interesting. Dufy made his tulips and anemones dance, Rennie Mackintosh emphasised their line. Look also at Odilon Redon's spellbinding flower pieces, where the individual flowers are most carefully spaced, often with large voluptuous blooms and delicate sprays juxtaposed in thrilling contrasts of scale and colour. Redon uses simple vases set against luminous backgrounds which emphasise the decorative shapes of the flowers. Certainly the flowers are the focal point of the picture, but what happens outside the vase is just as important in terms of the whole design.

In Marc Chagall's mysterious paintings the scale is more obviously manipulated. Great bouquets of flowers enfold diminutive pairs of lovers, while flying violinists glide across the background. 'The Painter and his Models' is a picture of himself working on a flower piece with large flowers floating around waiting to be arranged!

'Antique Flowers', one of John Nash's illustrations for The Curious Gardener *by Jason Hill (1932). This informal posy would adapt well as an embroidery design. Note the added interest of the mat pattern, and the flower and leaf on the table.*

Margaret River's 'Floral Street' (1991), was inspired by the bright mix of potted plants on a stall in Kingston market. It combines hand and machine embroidery on a ground of lightly sprayed silk noile.

(right) 'Amaryllis' by Janet Haigh, 1985. The idea came from seeing the plant on the floor of a marbled bathroom where the colours matched those of the amaryllis in intensity. The flower is in long and short stitch in filament silk, and the ground is hand-marbled silk, pieced in patchwork in diamonds and applied in squares with machine whip stitch.

In needlework arrangements similar liberties can be taken with scale, and full decorative use made of the background. I nearly always start a design with flowers picked from my garden or bought for the purpose, but I often place them in settings which are partly or even wholly imaginary: my needlework becomes an opportunity for vicarious living as I prop up an illustration of a Japanese screen or a postcard of a coveted painting as a make-believe background for my flowers. Equally effective might be a sheet of wrapping paper, wallpaper or a furnishing sample, provided the design is not too 'busy'. Only suggestions of shape and tone are needed, which can be painted, sprayed or stencilled on the ground. An alternative is to use dress or furnishing material, or to pattern a plain fabric with stitches as Val Tulloch has done in her anemone pictures (see p104).

Fallen petals make subsidiary patterns, and so do small objects such as shells, a pincushion or some reels of thread. Once you start composing simple still-lifes with flowers for embroidery, the process can become addictive. Try putting together two or three little pots of crocus and dwarf iris with a vase holding a few snowdrops and the scissors used to cut them, and see how easily you can build up a design. Choose the pots or cache-pots with care; as with cut flowers, the appearance of a pot plant can be completely altered by its container.

Still-lifes make ideal subjects for pictures or small screens, whereas a plant in a pot is equally well suited for furnishing designs, especially cushions. Just one dramatic flower stem can be effective – look at the amaryllis, and also the auricula: as Parkinson so charmingly described it 'seeing that their flowers, being set together upon the stalke, do seeme every one to be a Nosegay alone of itselfe'.

Auricula Ursi flore mixtu eflavo
& fusco rubro coloris.

Türickel mit gelb und dunckel roth geflecktten blumen.

An auricula in a pot from G. W. Knorr's Thesaurus Herbariae Hortensusque Universalis *(1750–72).*

106

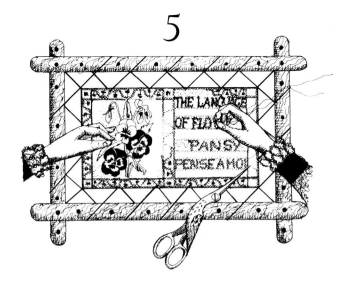

5

THE LANGUAGE
OF FLOWERS

SOME SACRED FLOWERS

Of all sacred flowers the Madonna lily – 'the plant and flower of light', symbol of purity and the emblem of the Virgin – is the best known. In embroidery it appears on the fourteenth-century binding of the Felbrigge Psalter, the earliest needle-work book cover to survive, now in the British Library. This belonged to the nun Anne de Felbrigge, and it is probable that she herself worked the charming Annunciation on the upper cover. Here, between the angel and the Virgin, is a lily in a gold vase banded in blue, bearing flowers so formalised they resemble fleurs-de-lis rather than lilies and, curiously, they are faintly tinged with red, who knows for what reason.

The Annunciation was one of the favourite scenes depicted on the magnificent vestments made by the medieval embroiderers and worn in the great cathedrals. A fine example can be seen in the Butler Bowden cope in the Victoria and Albert Museum, and in another scene on this sumptuous vestment the Virgin is depicted in a golden gown embroidered with a single red rose, symbol of divine love. Sacred roses, lilies and the columbine – associated through its bird-like florets with the Dove of the Holy Spirit – continued to appear on vestments until such work was brought to a halt at the Reformation, but their association with the Christian virtues (and before that with pagan superstitions and flower lore) was too deeply embedded for them to be altogether forgotten, and their descendants can be traced in patterns in seventeenth-century samplers.

Then in the nineteenth century, the beauty and symbolism of the medieval vestments were rediscovered by designers like Morris and Pugin, who studied the copes and were greatly inspired by their matchless technique and dignified designs. In contrast to the naturalistic rendering of 'hearts, roses and doves . . . better suited to valentines' in Berlinwork

*The Girlhood of Mary Virgin'
by Dante Gabriel Rossetti. The
completed embroidery can be
seen in Rossetti's Annunciation
painting 'Ecce Ancilla Domini',
also in the Tate Gallery.*

(right) *Madonna Lily (*Lilium
candidum*) from L. Fuch's de
Historia Stirpium (1542).*

(far right) *Modern Gothic lily
panel from* Nature in Ornament
by L. F. Day.

(far left) *The Felbrigge Psalter, a thirteenth-century manuscript in a fourteenth-century binding worked mainly in split stitch in coloured silks on a gold ground.*

(left) *The Virgin on the Butler Bowden cope, drawn by Sarah Siddall to show the fanciful treatment of daisies and oak leaves in the design. The cope was embroidered in gold and coloured silks on red velvet in about 1330.*

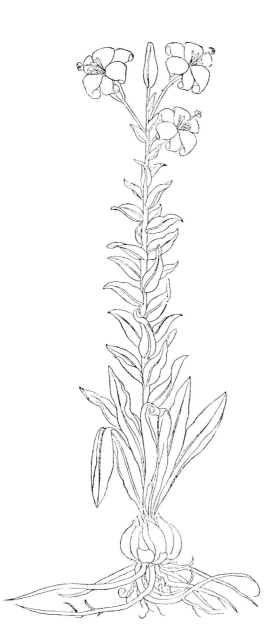

made for the church, Pugin extolled the refinement and elegance of the medieval flowers. These qualities can be seen in the Madonna lily in Dante Gabriel Rossetti's 'The Girlhood of Mary Virgin' – one of the loveliest of all paintings recording the quiet pleasure of embroidery. It depicts the Virgin seated at a frame, stitching the flower under the watchful eye of her mother Saint Anne; she has finished the three blooms and is now at work on the leaves and stem, her gaze directed at the real lily in the pot before her. The picture was first shown in 1849 when books on floral symbolism, both religious and secular, were extremely popular – deciphering the complex meanings in the picture would therefore have added to its appeal. Rossetti's contemporaries would have recognised the convolvulus as the symbol of humility, and the rose in the vase as the symbol of divine love.

(above and right) *Stewart Merrett's 'Heritage for Visions' panels (1985) trace the development of the pomegranate from bud to maturity. The details in the colour illustrations show the flower, and also the ripe fruit whose many seeds symbolise the countless souls within the Christian Church and their hope of Eternal Life. The motifs are applied in silk, satin and velvet on a gold ground. The pomegranate was popular in sixteenth- and seventeenth-century needlework, and reappeared during the Gothic Revival in the designs of many ecclesiastical embroideries.*

With the exception of the rose, the Virgin's flowers were traditionally white and blue; however, in one of the freshest and most moving sacred scenes in embroidery the emblematic flowers are joined by spring bulbs and plants in a whole range of bright colours. This is the 'Nativity' panel worked by Ann Macbeth for the little church at Patterdale in the Lake District where she spent her retirement. Here on one of her walks she came across a tiny manger in a ruined farm: 'It was just large enough to hold a tiny baby comfortably . . . and that set my needle going', she wrote later. The Virgin's hand rests on the manger and an angel – as marvellously decorative as any in the medieval vestments – is showing the Infant Jesus a symbolic Star of Bethlehem (*Ornithogalum umbellatum*). Spring flowers powder the ground where they kneel, among them Lady's Mantle (*Alchemilla mollis*), Lady's Slipper (*Cypripedium calceolus*), stitchwort and daisies, together with daffodils, bluebells and forsythia chosen for their festive colours and lively shapes. Most beautifully worked in wools with a little silk, the flowers express Ann Macbeth's reverence and delight in the scene.

(below right) *'The Nativity' by Ann Macbeth c1940, worked in multicoloured wools and silk on a linen ground with a border of blue and colourless glass beads. The background brings alive the village of Patterdale and the River Goldsill, with Helvellyn and Grisdale in the distance.*

(below) Alchemilla mollis *drawn by Richard Hatton in* The Craftsman's Plant-Book.

MORE THAN MEETS THE EYE

In Eastern Lands they talk in flowers,
And they tell in a garland their loves and cares;
Each blossom that blows in their garden bowers,
On its leaves a mystic language bears.

This verse was quoted in many nineteenth-century books about the 'language of flowers', and refers to the Turkish custom of conveying a message by sending certain flowers wrapped in an embroidered handkerchief. Lady Mary Wortley Montagu had first-hand experience of this when she was in Constantinople in 1718: replying to a lady who had asked for an example of such an unusual form of love letter, she wrote: 'There is no colour, no flower . . . that hath not a verse belonging to it; and you may quarrel, reproach and send letters of passion, friendship and civility without inking your fingers.'

The snake in the strawberry from Geoffrey Whitney's A Choice of Emblems.

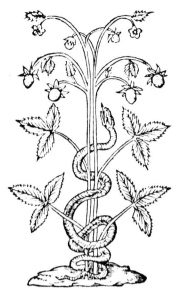

Dress trimming, c1600 worked with a message in coloured silks on mulberry satin slashed at the edges and ornamented with silk cord and French knots.

To send messages through flowers is an appealing idea suggestive of romance and mystery, and embroidery has always been the perfect medium for conveying messages of a personal and private kind. Imagine receiving on St Valentine's Day a dress trimming embroidered with eyes brimming over with tears and hearts pierced with arrows set between borage, marigolds and wild strawberries. In about 1600 the recipient would undoubtedly have been able to 'read' the embroidery for at that time many flowers, and colours too, had an emblematic significance, and men and women delighted in allegories and in posing and deciphering visual puzzles. The embroidered message may have been a simple avowal of love, or a plea for favours from a love-lorn gallant, but the choice of flowers linked with eyes and hearts suggests that there is more to it than one might first suppose.

Marigolds and the colour yellow were associated with jealousy (Chaucer described the figure of Jealousy wreathed with marigolds), and this too could be the meaning of the wild strawberry, well known through Geoffrey Whitney's *A Choice of Emblems*. Emblem books were all the rage on the Continent, and this was the first to be translated into English, in 1586 – it became an immediate best-seller. Each emblem comprised a picture, a verse and a motto; in Whitney's book the strawberry appears with a snake hiding under its leaves, the motto 'the Adder lurketh privily in the grass', and a warning in rhyme against falling for flattery and 'sugared words'. Motto and image formed a 'speaking picture' which anyone familiar with these matters would

recognise and understand, whether they saw it embroidered on a gentleman's nightcap or ornamenting a silver cup, or heard it alluded to in conversation.

Therefore the gallant who commissioned the dress trimming for St Valentine's Day might have chosen the motifs and had them embroidered as a plea to his mistress to reject a suspected rival; but it is equally possible that they were worked by a lady as an expression of *her* feelings of love and jealousy, and worn to advise her gallant of *her* plight.

The pattern-drawers at the Royal Exchange were quite accustomed to requests for designs incorporating amorous messages, and were adept at producing patterns for items such as caps and handkerchiefs; a good example would be the handkerchief embroidered with strawberries which Othello gave to Desdemona, and which she dropped with such fatal consequences. At first sight the choice of strawberries seems a curious one – surely mulberries, the badge of el Moro, the Moor, would have been more appropriate? But the wild strawberry was not only associated with rivals and jealousy; it was also well known as an emblem of purity, while its habit of flowering and fruiting at the same time made it irresistibly decorative and lastingly popular in needlework. The succulent berries in the sampler illustrated bring to mind Shakespeare's reference to sampler-making in *Pericles* and to the lifelike embroidery of flowers, where Marina

With her needle composes
Nature's own shape, of bud, bird, branch and berry
That even her art sisters the natural roses . . .

Sampler, early seventeenth century, worked with strawberries, pansies and roses in detached buttonhole stitch in coloured silks and gold; the small patterns would also be suitable for pincushions and sweet bags. Note the bird, apparently eating a slug.

Sixteenth- and seventeenth-century strawberry motifs.

Queen Elizabeth wearing a magnificent gown with flowers in blackwork in an anonymous portrait painted in 1590. Her favourite heartsease is pinned to her ruff, and she wears a strawberry on her stomacher. A pair of cherries dangles from her wig, and she holds a thistle – its embroidered counterpart can be seen worked on her sleeve.

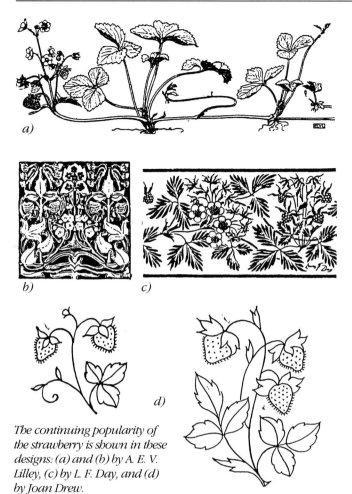

The continuing popularity of the strawberry is shown in these designs: (a) and (b) by A. E. V. Lilley, (c) by L. F. Day, and (d) by Joan Drew.

At court Shakespeare would have appreciated the magical effect of flowers embroidered on dress; he would also have been familiar with happy domestic scenes like the one described by Helena in *A Midsummer Night's Dream* when she reminds Hermia of their closeness in childhood:

> We, Hermia, like two artificial Gods
> Have with our needles created both one flower,
> Both on one sampler, sitting on one cushion . . .

Just such a scene greeted Queen Elizabeth when she visited Bisham in 1592, where a pastoral entertainment had been devised by Lady Russell; it opened with her daughters Anne and Elizabeth dressed up as shepherdesses, busily working roses, eglantine and pansies in the Queen's stitch on their samplers. The flowers were symbolic of the Queen's virtues – she was constantly celebrated as the 'Tudor rose' and 'eglantine' (see Chapter 7), and the heartsease, or pansy, was associated with chastity and was her favourite flower. Lady Russell could not afford the ruinously expensive and elaborate entertainment put on by some courtiers for the Queen during her summer progresses; she had to think of a less costly way of engaging her attention, and to present her daughters at their needlework was a most happy thought, as the Queen was an accomplished embroiderer with a keen eye for emblematic suggestion. Sure enough, she responded most favourably to Lady Russell's inspired divertissement.

Pansies ornamented many of Queen Elizabeth's gowns – none more lifelike than the tiny plant on her stomacher in the famous 'Rainbow' portrait at Hatfield House. They were often embroidered in blackwork, although here the pansy is rendered in coloured silks in long and short stitch, together with cowslips and other bright flowers, symbolising the eternal spring brought about by the Queen's reign. These are flowers embroidered with a public rather than a private meaning; another example is the thistle, the emblem of Scotland, which ornaments the magnificent red velvet suit worn by Lord Seton, comptroller of Mary Queen of Scots' household, in a portrait in the Scottish National Portrait Gallery in Edinburgh. The Queen of Scots herself embroidered thistles for Bothwell when she was held prisoner at Lochleven, and they appear on either side of her monogram in one of the panels in the Oxburgh hangings. In a cushion at Hardwick Hall she has intertwined them with the rose of England and the lily of France, as if to comment on the entangled political web in which she was caught. Needlework played an important role in her life; in 1574 she sent as a gift to Queen Elizabeth a petticoat of red satin that she had worked herself with roses, lilies, pinks and honeysuckle – maybe, like Lady Russell, she had hoped that thereby she would find favour with the Queen through their mutual interest in embroidery.

Devising a royal gift was an exacting and worrying business, as it had to stand out from the vast number presented each year. Bess of Hardwick chose the Queen's favourite pansies for a professionally embroidered cloak of blue satin, and she may herself have worked the heartsease on the gown worn by the Queen in the portrait in the Long Gallery at Hardwick Hall. The motifs were worked on a white ground – this was the most fashionable colour at court at the end of the century when the portrait was painted.

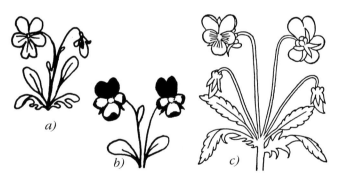

Pansy motifs (a) on Queen Elizabeth's stomacher in the Rainbow portrait, and (b) on the skirt in the Hardwick Hall painting, with woodcuts from (c) La Clef des Champs.

Colours as well as flowers had symbolic meanings, some of them reaching back to pre-Christian times. Everyone knew that when the Queen wore white lilies they signified purity, and many would have associated black with sorrow, constancy and death, green with youth and red with power. But during the sixteenth century, due to the increasing interest in heraldry, the significance of colours and what they meant became far more complex. There were books which described the precise meanings of every shade and combination of colour, but all sorts of problems arose when rival authors suggested conflicting meanings for the same colour;

for example the trimming illustrated on p112 was embroidered on mulberry satin: in one book this meant dissimulation, in another sadness, and in a third it meant peaceful love.

That lovers really did use the language of flowers in their dress to express their feelings and to carry on wordless conversations can be seen in plays and poems; and undoubtedly it added another dimension to the pleasures of embroidery, as in this mournful verse written by a lady abandoned by her husband:

> Give me black silk, that sable suites my hart,
> And yet som white, though white words do deceive,
> No green at all, for youth and I must part,
> Purple and blew, fast love and faith to weare.
> Mayden, no more sleepless Ile go to bedd,
> Take all away, the work works in my head.

We can only guess at the message implied in the choice of white satin for a pair of gloves worked with eyes shedding tears on pansies: white signified chastity and so did the pansy, but the flower was also used as a love charm; Shakespeare called it 'Cupid's flower' or 'Love-in-idleness', and in *A Midsummer Night's Dream* its juice was the love-charm laid on Titania's eyes.

The glove's message remains mysterious, and that is part of its appeal; its fascination goes far beyond its intricate stitchery, drawing us into the lives of men and women for whom embroidery was not only beautiful, but meaningful, pleasurable and totally absorbing.

FLORA'S ABC

In the diary he kept in the 1870s the engaging young curate Francis Kilvert wrote of finding a bookmark embroidered with a forget-me-not: 'It was a gift from a childhood sweetheart. But from which? I gazed at it conscience-stricken. Forget-me-not, and I had forgotten.'

There is little doubt that his sweetheart found her inspiration for the bookmark in one of the many sentimental books on the language of flowers which became a cult during the nineteenth century. Titles such as *Floral Emblems* (by Henry

Phillips, 1825), or *The Poetical Language of Flowers and Pilgrimage of Love* (by Thomas Miller, 1859) suggest that they were the descendants of the renaissance emblem books. They were certainly related to the nostalgic renewal of interest in a romantic courtly past (as seen in Sir Walter Scott's novels), but whereas the emblem and natural history books used by the sixteenth- and seventeenth-century embroiderers had been enjoyed by a select circle of educated men and women, these new arrivals were intended to amuse a far wider – and largely feminine – readership. Whimsical rather than witty, these sentimental volumes followed the many books on botany and flower-painting which had become so popular at the end of the eighteenth century, and they reflect an ever-increasing interest in flower-growing, collecting and identification.

The ladies who bought the books undoubtedly read romantic stories and poems in magazines, which would also have provided them with patterns and ideas – for floral fancy work; for pressing flowers (especially those with some sentimental association, like those of a bridal wreath) and mounting them in albums; for botanising; and for drawing and painting flowers in watercolours. Some of the books were tiny dictionaries, listing the flowers and their meanings alphabetically; in others each flower was illustrated and described in verse or prose. The quality of the pictures and poems varied enormously, from the charming to the twee to the maudlin.

By far the most unusual and visually intriguing of these books was the earliest one of all, an *Abécédaire de Flore* which appeared in 1811, written by B. de la Chenaye and dedicated to Napoleon's second wife Marie Louise. It was also intended for embroiderers, and the full title explained its purpose – it was (and I translate) *Flora's ABC or the language of flowers, letters, syllables and words, followed by some observations on the emblems, devices and emblematic meanings of a great number of flowers*. Ninety-six flowers were chosen for their prettiness and were exquisitely illustrated; moreover each one represented a particular sound, either a consonant or a vowel so when the flowers were put together in garlands they made up words and small sentences. These were ingeniously 'punctuated' by pansy

'There's pansies, that's for thoughts' says Ophelia in the mad scene in Hamlet*. On this glove they are worked in metal threads.*

This emblem in Henry Peacham's Minerva Britanna *(1612) depicts a sorrowful eye dropping tears, a motif popular with embroiderers.*

plants – a plant bearing a single bud was a comma; one with a bud and an open flower was a semicolon; one with a single flower a full stop, and if it was topped by a dragonfly, it represented an exclamation mark! So although the flowers were described in botanical detail, with notes on cultivation, the main object of the book was not to extend the reader's horticultural knowledge: it was devised as a means of painting or embroidering phrases which would then serve to enrich the home with 'speaking tapestries' – a perfect method for creating unique needlework presents, enabling embroiderers to express their feelings in a highly personal way and to create heirlooms for future generations.

Undoubtedly pretty, these garlands of mixed flowers and fluttering butterflies would have been meaningless if the recipient of the message did not also have a copy of the book. In fact I have yet to trace an embroidery based on the *Abécédaire*, but certainly the idea is sufficiently intriguing to want to try it out – if only to send a message saying 'Thank you!' for some specially thoughtful gift. Part of the pleasure would lie in explaining the language to the recipient, and this I suspect may have been one of the reasons for the success of these books during the nineteenth century.

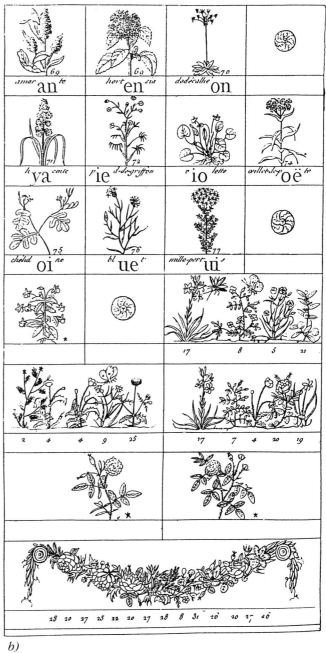

b)

Each flower represents a sound in B. de la Chenaye's ABC. The garland means 'Vous pouvez tout'.

Forget-me-not (a) from Flora's Feast *by Walter Crane (1899), and (b) from* The Craftsman's Plant-Book, *drawn by Richard Hatton.*

a)

117

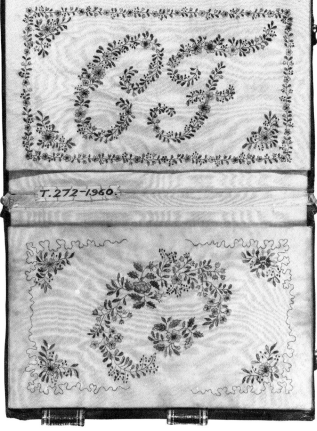

The lining of a pocket book in hairwork, c1836. The outer cover is beaded.

The title is written in flowers in J. J. Grandville's book: The Flowers Personified.

On the title page of The Beauties of Flora *a fairy places a handlight over an auricula.*

(right) *Bleuet and Coquelicot by Roy and Barbara Hirst (1990), inspired by the illustration in* The Flowers Personified. *This is an example of modern stumpwork, the figures padded and overlaid with calico, the skirts built up in layers of organza singed round the edges. The hats and bodices are in needlelace fragments which are applied to suggest the different parts of the flowers. The meadow grasses are in free machining on a ground of transfer-dyed organza over satin sheeting.*

118

A far more accessible but equally decorative floral language could be formed in embroidery simply by twisting the flower stems into the shape of letters, and ornamenting them with buds and leaves – as in the pocket book illustrated. This is hairwork, where a dark hair is used as an embroidery thread; this particular example is work of exceptional delicacy, enhanced by the cream watered silk of the ground. The idea could have come from the lettering on the title page of Samuel Curtis's *The Beauties of Flora* (1820). The illustration depicts Flora and a fairy in a magical setting reminiscent of *A Midsummer Night's Dream* – at the same time prefiguring the light-footed dancers of the romantic ballet.

It was one of these captivating ballerinas who inspired the equally romantic title page to J. J. Grandville's *The Flowers Personified* (1847), where the title is ingeniously written in flowers and tendrils. The book relates how the flowers are bored with being everlastingly used as emblems and subjects for poetry, and persuade the flower fairy to let them try living as humans for a change. Grandville illustrates their adventures, devising for each of them a wonderfully fanciful costume which brings out not only their 'human' but their 'flower' character at the same time. Thus in the opening story the brunette field poppy Coquelicot, and the fair-haired cornflower Bleuet have become shepherdesses, each with a young admirer and both happy in their new life – until their prettiness attracts as suitors an elderly judge and a squire. Hearing of this, their younger lovers desert them, and they are only saved from marriage with the two old men by the timely arrival of the Queen of France in the guise of their old friend the Lily.

Lady Ottoline Morrell's bedspread is worked mainly in long and short stitch in floss silks. The flowers include blue daffodils and carnations and turquoise roses.

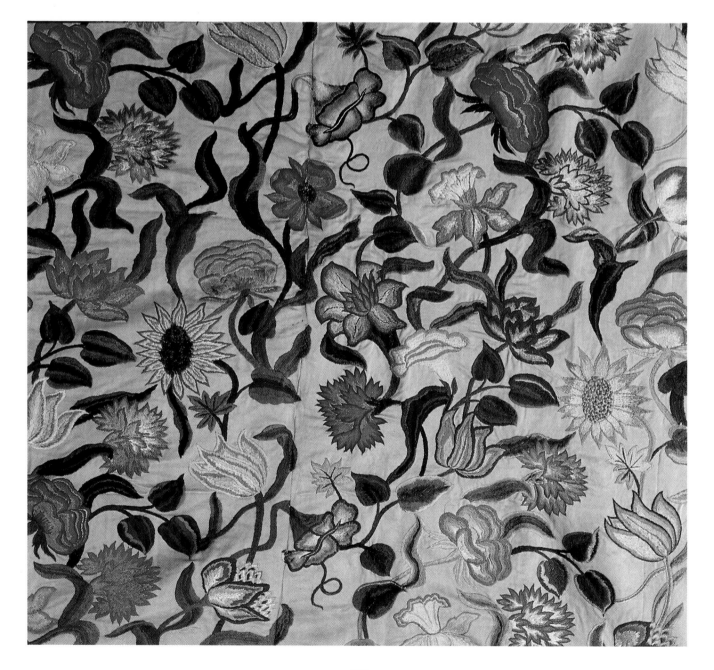

'BRIGHT WITH POETRY'

'One loves in flowers certain remembrances' wrote Alphonse Karr when introducing the stories in *The Flowers Personified*. It is certainly true that a particular flower will often straightaway evoke a person, a place or an occasion, and embroidery is a most satisfying medium in which to explore these associations. Karr's phrase came to mind as I read a passage written in 1915 by the charismatic Bloomsbury hostess Lady Ottoline Morrell, in her memoirs of her life at Garsington Manor near Oxford:

> I sat in my special chair under the lamp with a piece of embroidery and all my coloured silks spread out around me. Maria, when at home, sitting at my feet and perhaps she would be allowed to embroider a flower in one corner of the vast bedspread on which I was at work, Juliette at another corner. How much is woven in that coverlet! How intense the feelings as we worked at it. What interesting and vital ideas were blended with the silks and woven into the pattern of gay flowers. Some flowers must be bright with poetry, some dark and smudged with war; others vivid and bizarre with thoughts of life; and a lovely rose will always speak of the fragile beauty of love and friendship, and a sunflower was like one that grew in the garden with thoughts of Blake's 'weary of time'. Maria's flowers are red and sensual. Juliette's gay and multi-coloured, but perhaps rather *too* pretty.

In her autobiography *Leaves of the Tulip Tree* (1986), Juliette Huxley describes how in the evenings after dinner Lady Ottoline would crochet or embroider, 'smoking cigarettes and sucking peppermints', while Bertrand Russell read aloud from Saint-Beuve's *Causeries de Lundi* 'in his faultless accent, vividly, absorbingly'.

And what of the bedspread? Had it survived? Fascinated by Lady Ottoline's account, I began making enquiries as to the possible whereabouts of this 'coverlet of exploding flowers', and read more about its maker, her circle at Garsington, and her enthusiasm for needlework and garden-making. Virginia Woolf describes how Lady Ottoline 'mused at Garsington with her embroidery on her lap and her undergraduates at her feet . . . she created her own world'; and David Cecil remembers how Garsington was 'beautiful and a little shabby: and the shabbiness enhanced its beauty. It made it seem lived in – and ancient and dream-like . . . the garden was as romantically beautiful as the house.' Lady Ottoline loved the garden: 'I felt so happy watching the flowers – the brown ringed sunflowers, the red hot pokers, the phlox and montbretia, the zinnias and marigolds all crowded together in luxurious company.'

Through the kindness of Lady Ottoline's descendants I was eventually to see the sunflowers' embroidered counterparts on the bedspread, and it was as thrilling a moment as any needlework enthusiast could wish for. Here were the 'red and sensual roses', and with them a luxurious company of striped tulips, sumptuous peonies and Juliette's pretty multicoloured flowers – carnations and anemones as eye-catching as any florist's creation – all worked in brilliant glossy silks that were still startling in their intensity. These gorgeous threads have also been preserved, together with a wonderfully varied collection of embroideries assembled by Lady Ottoline and her mother-in-law Mrs Hariette Morrell, who was also a fine needlewomen.

A year later in 1915, Lady Ottoline worked another bedspread, this time as a present for D. H. Lawrence. It would be fascinating to speculate which flowers she chose for its design. Lawrence was an intermittent embroiderer himself (Lady Ottoline owned a phoenix made by his own hand) and he would have appreciated the time and thought spent on the gift; but sadly in his letter of thanks he makes no mention of the quilt's subject, merely telling Lady Ottoline that he and his wife Frieda 'would often lie on it and discuss its colourful design'.

In 1925 Lady Ottoline's husband Philip Morrell had a booklet printed, written by his mother Hariette Morrell, in which she had listed in detail all the embroideries she had made during her long life (she had died the year before at the age of ninety-one). This included a crewelwork bedspread, begun in 1879 and 'at last finished' and given to Philip in 1890. Almost all the items were made as gifts for friends and relatives – a wallflower cushion for her mother-in-law; waistcoats for her children; no less than thirteen book covers, several of them worked with flowers; and two pictures of pansies – one for her mother and one for Philip – worked in the language of flowers. The French for pansy is *pensée*; it also means 'a thought' and therefore sounds the same as the request *pensez* – Hariette had added the words *à moi* beneath each posy, thus making it read 'Think of me'.

Illustration of a vase of roses from Mrs Morrell of Black Hall, *a booklet describing the pieces of work she made between 1870 and 1924.*

PERSONAL PRESENTS

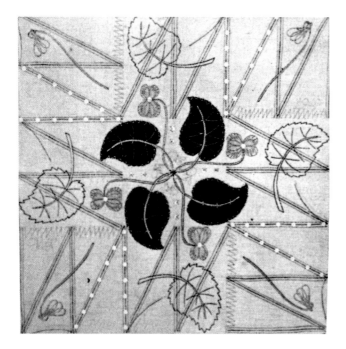

Personal pillow with violets and Vs in machine-stitched appliqué, by Lilian Dring.

Initials and flowers in Embroidery *(1909).*

Making presents for people we love is one of the great pleasures of embroidery, and the more personal they are, the more they are appreciated. However small and simple the gift may be – a bookmarker, pincushion or needlecase – if it is worked with the recipient's initials and bears their favourite flowers it is extremely satisfying both to plan and to make. The recipient's taste must be considered as much as your own, and this may lead to ideas and motifs you had not thought of before.

When letters and flowers are combined, the first essential is that they should work together and form an integrated design. It makes sense to begin with the letters, as their shapes are clear and precise. Look how Lilian Dring uses the angular letter 'V' to co-ordinate the design of a cushion made for Violet Mills. This was one of a series of 'personal pillows' made in the 1930s when Lilian Dring was making a name for herself as a designer. Her training in graphics and her instinctive feeling for lettering stood her in good stead when she became interested in embroidery. Few embroiderers have that advantage, but a great deal can be learned from looking at the ways in which flowers and letters were combined in the past – in printing for example. The letters in the 'sealed book' of Charles II (1661) were reproduced by Richard Hatton in *The Craftsman's Plant-Book* as examples of perfectly balanced decorative patterns, together with diagrams explaining how each one was devised. I have found these invaluable, either to use as they are, or as a blueprint for making up similar designs using different letters and flowers. The square shape makes them ideal for cushions or the tops of boxes.

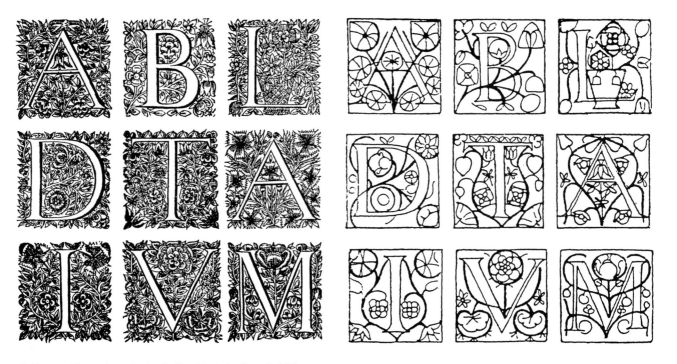

(left) *Initial letters from the 'sealed book' of Charles II (1661), and* (right) *Richard Hatton's analysis of them.*

Two boxes made and machine embroidered on Thai silk by the author (1991). The smaller is based on the 'sealed book' initial V, and the larger on the printer's device on this page.

The designs were quickly and accurately transferred to the cambric backing the silk by the simple method of using a photocopy, enlarged to the exact size of the lid, as a 'transfer'. First a solvent of one cup water, one cup white spirit and a few drops of detergent was brushed over both photocopy and cambric to dampen them. Then the copy was placed face down on the cambric and (protecting both it and the work surface with layers of old fabric or newspaper) firmly pressed over with a very hot dry iron to transfer the design. The author devised the waved band patterns on the sides of the boxes to include the flowers on the lids.

Note: these transfers are not washable and work best on cottons. The initials will need slight adjustment if worked, as here, from the back.

A sixteenth-century printer's device from The Craftsman's Plant-book *with some of the flowers drawn in detail.*

you can then get the scale exactly right for the size of cushion you plan to make. Small shallow boxes show off the embroidery most effectively, especially if you use light-reflecting materials like shot silk; they can be made with the sides plain, or with the motifs adapted either to fit each side panel, or as a continuous border, depending to some extent on how the box is to be made up. This is the trickiest part of the project, as a framework must be made both for the box and for the fabric-covered lining. Use a craft knife and set square to cut the top, base and sides from firm mount or matt card. For the box, the sides can be made either as four separate panels, or as a single length; cut no more than half-way through the card's thickness along the line where the card must bend round the base corner. For the lining, all the pieces should be cut very slightly smaller, and it is best to make the side panels separately. Make certain that the box and lining framework fit neatly together before lacing the embroidery and lining fabric firmly in place over the individual pieces. Slip stitch the sides and base of the box firmly together and glue the lining in place. Though fiddly, boxes are not difficult to make, but accuracy in measuring and cutting is essential. A box is more appealing if it contains a message or pretty surprise inside. Some flowers, such as

Pansy motif from Gerard's Herball

pansies, need no words to convey their meaning – a sprig worked on the lining of the base is all that is needed.

Other flowers attract us as much by their names as by their appearance. Meadowsweet, cranesbill, eyebright and many other equally affectionate and satisfying names go back to the sixteenth century, 'that period of supreme verbal happiness and strength' as Geoffrey Grigson called it. Some of the most attractive names were inspired by the tools and stitches of embroidery – 'thimbles flower' for example, was another name for both foxglove and columbine, and 'pins and needles' served for scabious *and* for gorse. Many of the names were regional; in Somerset, 'Lady's needlework' was stitchwort (*Stellaria holostea*) but elsewhere it could be cow parsley, hemlock or valerian. In *Some English Gardens* (1904) Miss Jekyll (see p2) describes valerian as 'Lady Coventry's needlework', explaining how 'short stitches and long would easily render the small divisions of the calyx and the long slender spur and single pistil'. 'Lady's pincushion' was vetch in one county, and teasel, lungwort, scabious and cornflower in others.

If the flowers originally inspired the names, these other suggestions found in books and regional dialect can surely be interpreted in needlework. No words or letters are needed, as the flowers speak for themselves. A pincushion might be worked with formalised scabious heads, the pins grouped together to form the centres, or with cornflowers which combine distinctive star and scale patterns. Camerarius's stitchwort would fill the cover of a needlebook with very little simplification; and taking the idea a stage further, the various 'Lady's needlework' flowers could be brought together to embellish a simple folding case for needles, pins and a small pair of scissors.

Consider also the 'Needlework' auricula and 'Embroidered Cranesbill' mentioned in Chapter 3 (see pp74, 76): these would be most suitable as subjects to enhance the cover of a small notebook, such a one as to slip in the pocket when visiting exhibitions, gardens or museums in order to make notes for future work – or to embellish the binding of a book in which embroideries already made are listed and described.

Valerian, known as 'Lady's needlework', drawn by Grace Christie.

A cornflower design from L. F. Day's Nature in Ornament *(1892) which could be used for a needlecase.*

A cornflower and saxifrage drawn by Grace Christie and combined in a design suitable for a book cover, from Needle and Thread *(1914).*

A woodcut of stitchwort in J. Camerarius's Epitome Matthioli *(1586) inspired this needlecase.*

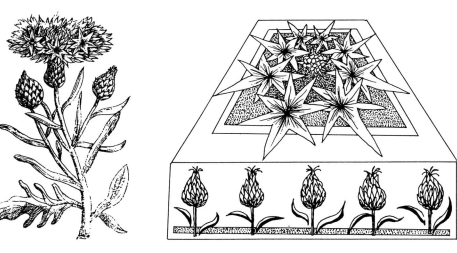

Pincushion inspired by this illustration of a cornflower in Sweert's Florilegium *of 1612.*

6

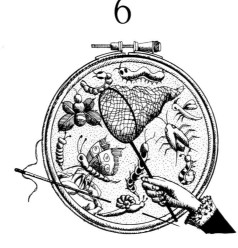

'SUNDRYE SORTES OF FLIES, BEASTES AND WORMES'

THE TULIP AND THE BUTTERFLY

The tulip and the butterfly
Appear in gayer coats than I:
Let me be.dressed as fine as I will
Flies, worms and flowers exceed me still.
Doctor Isaac Watts

The sight of butterflies, bees and birds busy among wild and garden flowers adds immeasurably to our delight in them. Rivalling the flowers in subtlety of colour and texture, their varied shapes and patterns have always attracted the attention of artists, many of whom have tried to capture the happy companionship that exists between them. There are charm-

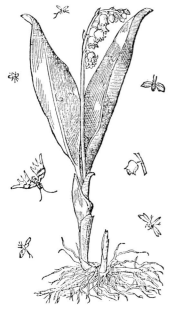

Lily-of-the-valley surrounded by insects in D'Alechamps' Historia Generalis Plantarum *(1586–7).*

ing examples in the borders of illuminated manuscripts, but nowhere are they more endearingly rendered than in the needlework of the sixteenth and seventeenth centuries.

The embroiderers of those days had a particular fondness for creepie crawlies, and gave no more attention to butterflies whose beauty has kept them permanently in favour, than to far less obvious subjects (to us, at least) such as worms, snakes and centipedes. Queen Elizabeth found these much to her taste, and her wardrobe included gowns glittering with flies, worms, grasshoppers and spider webs; oddest of all was a lacy shawl embellished with a life-like black spider. And it was clearly because he knew such things pleased her that in 1580 Lord North spent the large sum of fifty shillings to have a pair of gloves embroidered with 'Froggs and Flies' as a gift for her.

Occasionally these creatures were chosen because they had meanings – in the 'Rainbow' portrait at Hatfield, Queen Elizabeth wears the serpent of wisdom on her sleeve, while snakes, frogs, bees and butterflies appeared again and again in the emblem books. However, their immense popularity in embroidery can be explained partly because they looked so decorative in book illustrations, and partly because of the contemporary delight in the natural world and all its inhabitants. Fauna was as fascinating as flora, and the spiral patterns on a snail shell were as intriguing as the radiating florets of a honeysuckle. Snails peering out inquisitively from their shells were particular favourites. In *Venus and Adonis* Shakespeare gives a 'snail's eye view' of what happens when its horns are touched and it retreats into its shelly cave:

And there all smothered up does sit
Long after fearing to creep forth again.

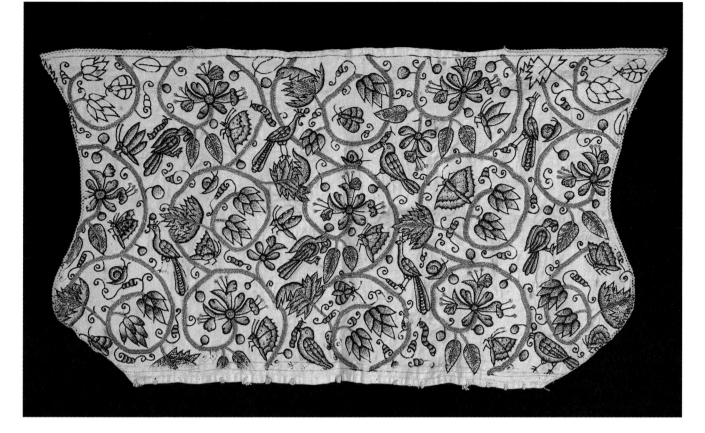

(above) *A coif in blackwork c1600, embroidered with birds, snails and insects in speckling stitches. The coif would have been seamed along the top to form a cap shape.*

Two snails from Conrad Gesner's natural history Icones Animalium *(1560).*

(above) *Early seventeenth-century pillow cover worked in coral stitch in black silk with worms, butterflies and snails which reappear in the coiling stem of the border.*

Snails, insects and deer in a pattern by Thomas Trevelyon.

His description is sensitive and affectionate at the same time, and these qualities are often evident in needlework too, the embroiderer not only trying to render the creature's likeness, but to suggest something of its character as well.

Of all creatures, bees were the most loved. Sugar was then an expensive luxury, and honey was the principal source of sweetening, so few households would have been without a hive or two, and the bees, like the flowers, were generally tended by the housewife. Small wonder, then, that they appear so frequently in stitchery. The medley of flowers in nosegay gardens and knots also attracted butterflies in profusion:

> There lavish Nature in her best attire
> Powres forth sweet odours and alluring sights . . .

wrote Edmund Spenser, following the flight of a butterfly from one flower pattern to another, led by its 'curious busy eye'. The embroiderers rarely attempted to depict butterflies realistically; instead they liked to speckle bodies and wings in blackwork, stripe them in bands of colour, or pattern them in silver gilt and spangles.

Insects were equally popular as subjects for dress and furnishings. The professional embroiderer in the anonymous play *Sir Giles Goosecap* (1606) was working an entire set of bed-hangings with 'nothing but glow-worms' – their likeness was presumably achieved with 'glistering gold' and spangles, and the effect was so brilliant that no other lights were needed in the bedchamber.

As companions for flowers, birds appealed almost as much as insects. Jaunty blackbirds and fat parrots were depicted in books with flowers and animals, some bigger,

Latiné VERDON. Gallicé VERDIER. Latiné LVSCINIA. Gallicé ROSSIGNOL.
Ger. GRVNLING. An. GREENFINCHE. Ger. NACHTGALL. Ang. NIGHTINGALE.

Lat. PICA, GLANDARIA. German. GAY. Latiné VLVLA. Gallicé HVLOTE.
German. HAHER. Anglicè IAY. German. EVL. Anglicè OWLE.

Bird designs in La Clef des Champs *(1586) and* (right) *A bird in a pansy from* A Scholehouse for the Needle *(1632).*

(right) *Squirrel from a late seventeenth-century crewelwork curtain, showing stem stitch used as a solid filling and a butterfly in buttonhole stitch worked as an open filling from* Embroidery and Tapestry Weaving *by Grace Christie (1906).*

(left) *A kingfisher and fritillaries from L'Anglois'* Livre des Fleurs *(1620).*

Disproportionate scale was a feature in many seventeenth-century pattern-books, as can be seen in this page from Thomas Johnson's A Booke of Beasts, Birds, Flowers and Fruit *(1630).*

some smaller than themselves, designed to be plucked from the page, and transferred in outline to satin or twill with total disregard for naturalistic scale. In the process of copying, some birds and insects – and animals, too – acquired even more human expressions, and stumpwork and crewelwork abound in smiling, jaunty, and occasionally glowering creatures. Birds perching in trees and flowers were as pleasing in needlework as in the real garden – especially the nightingale which 'will help you to cleanse your trees of Caterpillars and all noysome wormes and flies' according to William Lawson in *A New Orchard and Garden* (1618).

By the seventeenth century, native birds and flowers were joined by chinoiserie and other entirely imaginary creations, devised by the pattern drawers to amuse their patrons. It may have been this type of design that in 1664 caused a lady of the Verney family, engaged on a crewelwork curtain, to complain: 'There is certain birds and flyes and other creepers which I do not know, and frutes that I do not like'; there was altogether 'too much work in it', and it must have been a relief when she found it still 'a very fine thing though they be left out'. Some birds soon became clichés, like the parrot on a cherry sprig (see pp5,18), but other little creatures like squirrels always looked engaging, and their popularity in embroidery perhaps reflects the vogue then for keeping them as pets, enjoyed as much by adults as by children.

Accurately observed Pink Emperor Gum Moth newly hatched from its cocoon and depicted in its natural habitat of coral heath, grasses and branches by Annemieke Mein

(1982). Worked in machine and hand embroidery on a painted ground in various threads including unravelled carpet wool.

WONDROUS TRANSFORMATIONS

The artists whose designs appealed most to embroiderers generally juxtaposed flowers, birds and butterflies for no other reason than that they enhanced each other; however, this was not the case in the exquisite illustrations made by Maria Merian in her book *The Wondrous Transformation of Catterpillars (Erucarum ortis)* (1718). In these, the flowers were chosen because they were the food plants of the insects whose 'wondrous transformation' into butterflies and moths was the subject of the book. Maria Merian's interest in entomology (then an entirely new science) began when, as a child, she reared silkworms on mulberry leaves; eventually it took her to the remote jungles of Surinam in South America to draw and study tropical insects. She married at eighteen but was soon separated from her husband, and began doing embroidery in order to support herself. In a *Memoir* written in 1846, James Duncan tells us that 'she handled the needle with as much skill as she did her pencil, her productions being distinguished by an elegance and delicacy of execution which made them resemble paintings'.

This mulberry garland in Maria Merian's The Wondrous Transformation of Caterpillars *would adapt well as a design for a book cover.*

(right) Waistcoat c1780 *worked with insects in coloured silks on a satin ground.*

*Pale tussock moth on a
dandelion by Maria Merian.*

Maria Merian makes her subjects decorative as well as scientifically correct, a talent which probably developed while she was devising her needlework designs, and it is this aspect of her work that makes her so fascinating for embroiderers. In her engraving pictured here, see how the patterns echo and complement each other in the rectangular shapes of the dandelion petals and the tufts on the pale tussock moth.

Generally, study of the natural world expanded during the eighteenth century – a nice example originates from the enterprising Richard Hoy who in 1778 was advertising glass beehives which ladies could study on their dressing tables 'without the least fear of being stung'; however, in spite of this trend, the embroiderers of the period seem gradually to have lost interest in the insect world, and the number of small creatures depicted accompanying flowers was much reduced. Exotic birds and butterflies remained in favour, darting among peonies and chrysanthemums as brilliant as those on Chinese wallpapers, but it was only on waistcoats, in particular those designed in France, that a rich variety of insects was to be seen, together with charming motifs of cocks and hens, rabbits and small monkeys.

Delicate embroidery on full dress suits continued to be worked in France until the Revolution and the fall of the French monarchy, and a most poignant relic of that period is preserved in the Musée Carnavalet in Paris: a pincushion in the shape of a butterfly, that supreme symbol of the fragility of human life, made from the fragments of a cornflower-embroidered waistcoat worn by Louis XVI during his imprisonment in the Temple in 1792–3. There, Marie Antoinette and her daughters spent many hours at their embroidery in an attempt to make the time pass more

quickly, until even their needlework tools were taken away; it has never been discovered whether the pincushion was made by the King's daughter, the Duchesse d'Angoulême, or by one of his devoted servants.

FLOWERS AND PETS

It is hard to imagine a more perfect partner for the showy flowers of Berlin woolwork than the gaudy family of parrots, and many nineteenth-century parlours boasted a screen or picture depicting them in the brightest colours in tent stitch or in plushwork, which exaggerated their sleek curves. The designs often came from the magnificent bird books of the 1830s and 1840s, most notably from Edward Lear's *Illustrations for the Family of Psittacidae or Parrots* (1830–2).

Like Maria Merian, Lear depicted his subjects in minute and accurate detail, and he, too, made them look splendidly decorative – the ornamental nature of his parrots, which were drawn from life in London Zoo, was immediately spotted by the Berlin designers. They seized on the boldness of the outlines, unperturbed by the fact that the subtlety of the plumage could never be rendered on canvas, however fine. Lear's declining eyesight ruled out further drawing of this meticulous kind, and he turned to the greater freedom offered in watercolour painting, travelling the world in search of subjects and writing his inimitable *Nonsense Verses*. The plants in *Nonsense Botany* (1871), incongruously sprouting people, birds and insects, have much in common with the curious hybrids of stumpwork where flowers and birds have human faces; their carefree gaiety would make them intriguing subjects for children or adults to embroider.

May Morris had exactly this quality in mind when she wrote in an article in *The Art Workers' Quarterly*, 1902: 'Home made needlework should be irresponsible, gay, a little absurd sometimes and very personal.' She was reflect-

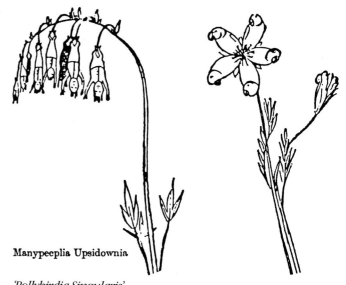

Manypeeplia Upsidownia

*'Pollybirdia Singularis',
'Cockatooca Superba' and the
well known 'Many Peeplia
Upsidownia' from Lear's
Nonsense Botany (1871).*

Pollybirdia Singularis

A cockatoo in plushwork perched on a basket of flowers in wools and silk in cross stitch c1850. Note the cabbage roses, auricula and a striped tulip with the rounded shape recently made fashionable by the florists.

Cockatooca Superba

ing on the charms of stumpwork, but she might almost have been describing some of her own embroideries, especially those in which birds, butterflies and small animals feature in the design. Like her father, she drew inspiration from the flora and fauna in Gothic tapestries and seventeenth-century crewelwork. The Elizabethan coiling stem patterns, alive with pert creatures, also appealed to her imagination and in the 'Owl' hanging she adapted them to suit her purpose, adding her own witty touches as she did so.

Happily the tradition of rendering the companionable spirit that exists between flora and fauna continues today, and humour still pervades the work of some contemporary embroiderers. In Belinda Pollit's picture, the dog statuesque on the balustrade is apparently basking in the flowers'

admiration. The dog can trace its needlework pedigree back to two sources: the affable pet spaniel tripping up the footman in the tea party scene depicted in the Stoke Edith hangings at Montacute; and the smirking spaniel seated by its owners which features in the Bradford table carpet in the Victoria and Albert Museum. A number of furnishings in the museum record the renaissance passion for pets, and none is more moving than the small dog – the symbol of friendship – worked by Mary Queen of Scots in an emblematic panel. However precarious her situation, she could still make witty comment on it – as, for example, when she embroidered herself as a mouse running dangerously near the claws of a cat whose ginger fur identifies it as Queen Elizabeth in feline form.

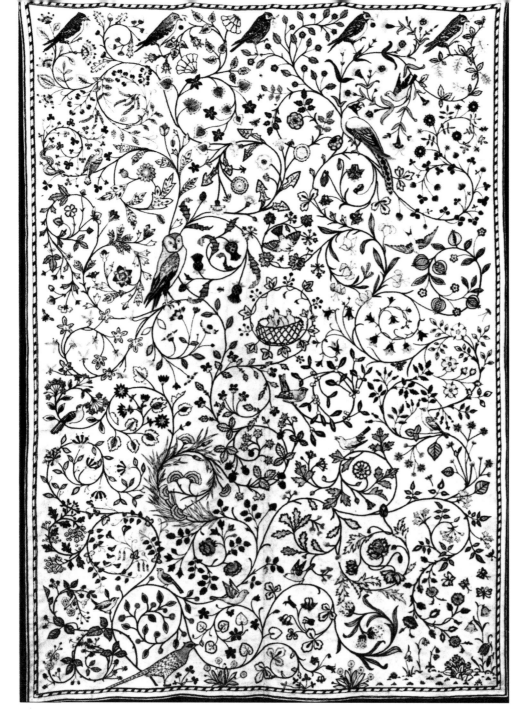

May Morris c1906 and worked in wools on linen by the students and teachers at the Birmingham Municipal School of Art.

(right) 'Dog Balustrade' by Belinda Pollit 1987: hand embroidery using variegated lace threads, stranded cottons and floss silk. The marble effect of the dog statue and balustrade is achieved by the use of shadow quilting, padding the semi-transparent silk with flecked wool. This smoothness contrasts well with the rich build-up of textures in the flower border.

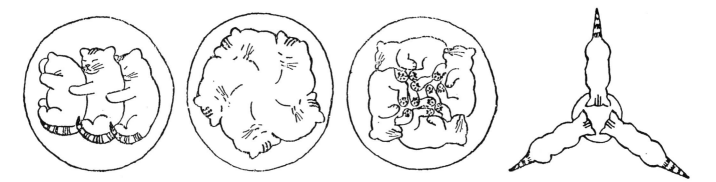

Kitten patterns in Children and Gardens *by Miss Jekyll.*

134

Cats seem to have an affinity with flowers, as Miss Jekyll noted in her beguiling book *Children and Gardens* (1908), charmingly illustrated with photographs of cats taking possession of her flower baskets and delighting in catmint. 'My garden' she wrote, 'would not be half the pleasure it is to me without the pussies . . . they are perfect garden companions.' Cats seem to have a knack of arranging themselves among flowers so decoratively that like Miss Jekyll, we find ourselves reluctant to disturb them.

Jennifer Wilson's 'Keats and Flowers' records a favourite cat happily ensconced in a border bright with poppies, lupins and iris. Her picture reminds me of an observation made by Nan Fairbrother about flowers and pets which in some curious way seems equally relevant to embroidery: 'Growing flowers is very much like keeping animals . . . to their keeper they become individual creatures whose health and happiness are his loving concern . . . The real gardener is paternal about his flowers, they are his pets.'

(below) *'Keats and Flowers' by Jennifer Wilson 1989: hand and machine embroidery on a calico painted ground, with fragments of transparent fabric* *applied by machining. A piece of black lace oversewn with straight stitches conveys the 'fuzzy' outline which was the hallmark of Keats'.*

BUTTERFLY BOXES

Insects, and butterflies in particular, invite simple pattern-making. The perfect symmetry of their shapes makes them easy to arrange in geometrical designs, and the intricate markings on wings and bodies suggest endless permutations of stitches and methods.

A single butterfly with its wings outspread might serve as a sampler for an experiment in outline, filling and raised stitches; or families of stitches – flat, looped, chained and knotted might be tried out on each of the wings. The bands and segments divide the wing space into attractive shapes; this is made clear in the diagram explaining the parts of a butterfly from *The Aurelian* by Moses Harris (1766). In any stitch, direction is all-important; in the wing segments, for example, try working the same stitch vertically, horizontally

or at an angle, using just one shade of stranded cotton or, better still, filament silk. This will create all sorts of variations in tone as the light catches the surface of the stitches. Many butterflies come in tawny shades, ideal for an experiment of this kind: by gradually adding one or two lighter and darker threads, you can convey the subtlety of the butterfly's marking whilst preserving the unity of the overall design.

In the process you will discover which stitches work best for you; these could then be developed further using the butterfly motif as the pattern for the lid of a box or a rectangular cushion. If you wanted to introduce flowers with the butterflies, follow Maria Merian's example and choose the insect's food plant as a border motif.

Two butterflies facing each other across a central flower

The Queen of Sheba by Frances Gibb, 1989, brings flora and fauna together in a 'kind of sampler' worked on an old-fashioned Singer 201 K treadle machine which the maker finds far more versatile than the modern swing-needle type. The subtlety of line and intricate patterning is achieved by skilfully 'throwing the stitch', a method which changes its direction very sensitively. The pale yellow organdie ground is cut through in places to reveal the intensity of the coloured silk motifs arranged behind it. Silk and gold threads add lustre, and so do the beads, strung on a long fluffy thread so they can be moved along and couched down by machine one at a time. The flowers were stitched from life or botanical prints.

A butterfly box in
The Aurelian *by Moses Harris (1766).*

make a pleasing design, and three might be arranged like the trio round a flower vase in the Oxburgh hangings. A quartet fits perfectly in a square cushion or box top with one in each corner, and this is easy to mark out accurately by pencilling along the diagonals on tracing paper and then making sure the bodies are aligned along them. The antennae can be arranged to form interesting subsidiary patterns if the motifs are placed close together, but you might prefer to introduce a central open flower-head like a dandelion. Any pocket butterfly book will provide a range of shapes and patterns which can be traced or photocopied, and if you want to experiment with more complex designs, these can be cut out and adjusted to make sure they are appropriate in scale and spacing for the project in hand.

Diagram to show the parts of a butterfly

A pair of butterflies adapted as a bookmark design from an illumination in the Hours of Anne of Burgundy *by Jean Boudichon; a trio of butterflies on a panel in the Oxburgh hangings, and a quartet of dragonflies suitable for a box-top or cushion.*

1. *Wood Tiger Moth*
2. *Cinnabar Moth*
3. *Crimson Speckled Footman*
4. *Caterpillar of D°*

Moths in The Naturalist's Library *(1846).*

Most pocket books, and those intended to assist in identification, present the butterflies with wings open and flat as if pinned ready to set in a case; this is ideal for formal, geometric types of design, but the butterfly's charm lies as much in the way it flutters about as in its colour and pattern, and to convey something of this a more random kind of design is needed. Photographs of insects hovering, alighting and feeding on the nectar of flowers provide an obvious source of motifs, and the engravings in some eighteenth- and nineteenth-century books are particularly useful because of their decorative intent. The extreme delicacy of moths, for example, is wonderfully rendered in the illustration from *The Naturalist's Library*, and it immediately suggests a treatment in the finest surface stitchery with minute beads.

(right) *'Frog Down Under' by Annemieke Mein, 1988. In this high-relief textile wall-sculpture the frog is padded and patterned in free machining, and the gum blossoms (*Eucalyptus sideroxylon*) are in French knots of varying size.*

(below) *Lily Pond Box by Belinda Montagu, 1988. The ripples on the pond are created by free machining, applied chenille, strips of leather and lines of beads on a ground of watered moiré; the lily pads are in leather and suede, and the toad and the fish are padded and ornamented with surface decoration in beads and gold threads. The dragonflies and bees are made with needlelace wings.*

Butterfly and bee chapter headings in The Garden's Story *by G. H. Ellwanger (1890).*

Insects in movement make wonderful subjects for three-dimensional objects like boxes, where their flight can be followed round the sides and onto the top. If metal threads and glinting beads are included in the stitchery they catch the light on the different surfaces and create a most lively effect. The fluidity of the machine-embroidered line is perfect for capturing insects in flight; worked at speed it has a spontaneity which is hard to match in hand work. When stitching the bodies, wings and antennae of dragonflies, or when following the tracery of a spider's web, try using increasingly fine silk, and gold or silver thread in the needle and bobbin of the machine respectively. If you slightly loosen the bobbin tension and wind it with silver thread, it will come to the surface in a series of minute dots resembling spangles of dew.

I remember coming upon a group of dew-laden spiders' webs sparkling in the early morning light on a hill path in Tuscany one September. Delicately suspended between tall growing poppies whose seed-heads were silhouetted against the sun, they were a target for any insect fluttering by; they were also the inspiration for a series of embroideries made on my return home. The first was a cushion with a poppy and spiderweb design worked on an ivory glazed chintz ground. The poppies and leaves were machined solidly in satin stitch in bright reds and greens on cambric, and then cut out and applied to the chintz, their bold shapes and colours contrasting with the fragility of the web which was machined in grey silk and metallic thread. The web was traced onto the transparent fabric – mull – which backed the chintz, and was worked from the wrong side so the intricate tracery could be followed easily with the needle.

The next projects were square and hexagonal boxes, the flowers worked on the sides and standing upright, support-

ing the web which embellished the lid. As on the cushion, a miscellany of small moths fluttered amongst the stems and circled the web. These motifs were repeated on a larger scale on an evening jacket in fine midnight-blue wool embroidered entirely in silver threads. Here the poppies were joined by cow parsley, and the flight of moths encircled the sleeves.

Poppy and spiderweb design for a cushion made by the author.

140

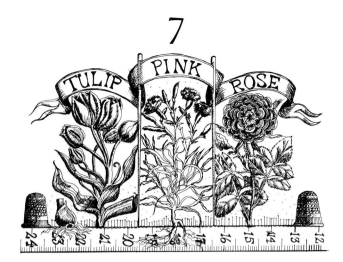

FAVOURITE FLOWERS

See how the Flowres as at Parade
Under their colours stand displaid:
Each regiment in order grows,
That of the Tulip, Pink and Rose.
'Upon Appleton House',
Andrew Marvell

ROSES

In 1598 the traveller Paul Hentzner visited Queen Elizabeth's library at Whitehall where he saw a number of magnificent books in red velvet bindings ornamented with pearls and precious stones. He does not single out any particular volume, so we do not know if he saw the rose-embroidered bible bound for her in 1583, now in the Bodleian Library in Oxford. The design is based on the Tudor rose, a formalised double flower composed of the white rose of York (*Rosa alba*) and the red rose of Lancaster (*Rosa gallica*), symbolising the union of the two royal houses in 1485 when Henry VII married Elizabeth of York. 'It is the honour and ornament of our English Scepter' wrote Gerard, and perhaps no flower has ever been so closely associated with an individual as the rose with Queen Elizabeth. Emblematic of the peace and prosperity brought by her rule, Tudor roses flourished in all the decorative arts – but in none did they find more varied expression than in embroidery.

Shortly before her accession, the Queen – then Princess Elizabeth – had visited her sister Mary Tudor at Richmond, travelling by water in a barge covered by a canopy of green silk embroidered with branches of eglantine and blossoms of gold. The eglantine was a prickly wild rose with 'glittering' scented leaves and (according to Gerard) 'most commonly

Stems of eglantine and Tudor roses intertwine on the red velvet binding of Queen Elizabeth's bible. The dual nature of the Tudor rose is emphasised by the double row of petals in silver gimp outlined in gold cord, their raised effect contrasting with the delicacy of the smaller eglantine in flat silk stitchery.

The formalised treatment of the Tudor rose makes it an ideal subject for embroidery, as the designs of (above) Joan Drew and (right and below) Thomas Trevelyon show.

Queen Elizabeth framed in Tudor and eglantine roses in the frontispiece to The Light of Britaine *by Henry Lyte (1588).*

whitish flowers'; though far less eye-catching than the Tudor rose, it had a particular appeal and significance for her. Emblematic of her purity and virginity, it is a constantly recurring motif, ornamenting at least three of her book covers and frequently mentioned as decorating items of dress and gifts listed in the royal inventories – for example the skirt of purple satin 'with roses of white lawn embraudered with gold'. These were probably three-dimensional flowers cut out and applied to create a delicate filmy effect, quite different from the sharply defined roses of blackwork or the stiff pearl-encrusted or detached button-hole blooms.

It is strange that the single and double yellow roses (*Rosa lutea* and *Rosa hemisphaerica*) introduced at the end of the sixteenth century were not taken up in seventeenth-century stumpwork or crewelwork; it would suggest that when choosing flowers for needlework, shape was sometimes of greater importance than colour. This was certainly the case in the moss rose, a mutant of the cabbage rose (*Rosa centifolia*) and which made its debut in Robert Furber's catalogue in 1730 (see illustration on page 96), appearing in embroidery soon afterwards. The 'moss' consisted of tiny hairs or glands which gave the stalks and sepals a furry look and extended the shape of the buds, making them an irresistible feature for embroiderers. Their attempts to render the mossiness in minute detached stitches can be seen in countless silk pictures and pole screens, many of which capture the beguiling daintiness of this type of rose, 'at once demure and picturesque' as Jason Hill so perceptively described it.

For rose enthusiasts, the early nineteenth century was a period of tremendous excitement, with hundreds of new varieties coming in, many of them in shades of brilliant red which quite eclipsed the blush tints of the previous century. They were collected and displayed in special rose gardens, massed in beds and festooned on ropes between pillars and over arches, in order to create the maximum decorative impact; this was exactly the effect the embroiderer had in mind when she juxtaposed the thrilling crimsons and scarlets of the new Bourbons and Hybrid Perpetuals like Great Western and Empereur du Maroc, working the different varieties in bouquets and garlands on separate squares of canvas which, when completed, were sewn together to make carpets or rugs, or even to cover a settee.

The new roses were not to everyone's taste, however. William Morris for example deplored the breeder's quest for size – ' . . . a florist's rose being about as big as a moderate Savoy cabbage' – and he disliked the coarseness that replaced the exquisite subtlety of form of the old roses. The cabbage rose had been a favourite with eighteenth-century embroiderers, who had succeeded in capturing its fragile charm in shaded silks and crewels; but now it was coarsely modelled in cross and plush stitch in Berlin wools so that it resembled the 'cabbage roses with solid rotundity of form' which garden writers like Forbes Watson found so distasteful. In his book *Flowers and Gardens* (1872), Watson championed the 'deeply satisfying charms of the Dog Rose', and

Cushion c1600, worked with a miniature tree bearing eglantine and double white roses on a silver ground.

'The Arms of Margaret Beaufort', a canvaswork panel by Mary Dickinson c1981, inspired by the entrance to St John's College, Cambridge which was founded in 1508 by Margaret Beaufort, mother of Henry VII. The red rose of Lancaster is worked in bullion knots in red crewel wool.

Cabbage rose in laid silk stitchery from Saint Aubin's L'Art de Brodeur (1770).

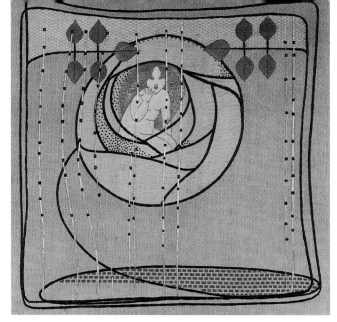

The distinctive linear qualities of the Glasgow style can be seen in Frances Macdonald's 'The Spirit of the Rose' c1900–5. The shape of the rose is applied in pink silk on linen with couching to suggest folded petals. The leaves are in satin stitch.

preferred the single and 'old-fashioned' flowers planted to show off their individual beauty rather than those displayed as 'blooming masses'.

Yet paradoxically some of Morris's richest designs are of cabbage roses: inspired by the medieval *Romaunt de la Rose* which describes the poet's search for love embodied in the perfection of the rose, his embroideries express 'the very essence of the rose's being' in a series of enthralling images. And how lush and exuberant these roses of Morris look in comparison with the innovative, pared-down shapes of Jessie Newbery's flowers, roses which were to become famous as the hallmark of the Glasgow style! A design for appliqué in her sketchbook drawn around 1900 (see p152) heralds the distinctive 'Glasgow rose' used on furniture,

Cabbage roses, 'the loveliest form of all', encircle the Heart of the Rose in this panel designed by William Morris and Edward Burne-Jones.

Worked in wool, silk and gold thread c1874–80, it formed part of the *Romaunt de la Rose* frieze made for Rownton Grange in Yorkshire.

'Olive and Rose' cushion cover from Embroidery Work (1912), a catalogue of Morris and Co designs.

glass and metalwork as well as on embroidered furnishings in the interiors of Charles Rennie Mackintosh (see p152). Startlingly different from the sentimental moss and cabbage roses of the previous age, her motifs looked fresh and stylish whether they were used on dress or furnishings, and they added elegance and individuality to the simple gowns she wore herself. In contrast to this purely decorative treatment, Frances Macdonald (a student at the School of Art in the 1890s, and sister-in-law of Charles Rennie Mackintosh) returned to the symbolism of the rose in the mysterious image embroidered in 'The Spirit of the Rose' pictured here.

In the early years of this century, the motif was endlessly imitated and adapted by Mrs Newbery's students and admirers, but seldom as successfully as by her assistant, Ann Macbeth who renewed its fading freshness in beautifully worked designs, such as sewn on the cushion illustrated on p152.

TULIPS: THE QUEENE OF BULBOUS FLOWERS

> Above and beyond all others, the Tulipas may be so matched, one colour answering and setting of another, that the place where they stand may resemble a peece of curious needlework . . .
>
> John Parkinson, 1629

Striped tulips from Parkinson's Paradisus.

Of all the new flowers introduced in the sixteenth century, it was the tulip that made the most spectacular entry in the European garden scene, and you have only to look at the early illustrations in books like Parkinson's to see why it excited such admiration. No other flower could match it in 'admirable variety of colour', and its shape too made it unique – at once elegant and sculptural, with a clarity of outline that was bound to delight embroiderers.

It was first cultivated in gardens in Turkey; in 1554 Ogier de Busbecque, the imperial ambassador to Suleiman the Magnificent, saw it there and determined to acquire bulbs of this wonderful flower. It reached England in 1578, and so had been cultivated in this country for fifty years by the time Parkinson admired his tulip bed and likened its effect to a 'peece of curious needlework' – a striking comparison, and one that immediately excites the embroiderer's curiosity.

Did he have a particular 'peece of needlework' in mind, and if so, how was it embroidered? The earliest needlework

Curtain c1650 with tulips, iris and fruit worked as slips in tent stitch and applied to a satin ground, with a subsidiary pattern of insects.

tulips appeared at the turn of the century in blackwork embroidered in speckling stitches which emphasised their shapely forms. This method was repeated in early crewelwork, but this too was monochrome, and as such could not have inspired the comparison. Turkeywork, much favoured for chair backs and seats, is a possibility, and there are some fine examples with tulips on them, but it is a carpet-knotting technique rather than a method of embroidery. However, from a distance it resembles canvaswork, and Parkinson may well not have differentiated between the two. On the other hand he would certainly have been familiar with furnishings ornamented with tent-stitch slips (see page 33), and these would seem to be the most likely candidates for his comparison. Using this method the clear-cut shapes could be rendered most effectively, as can be seen in the detail of the cream satin curtain pictured; its design is composed of a collection of striped tulips neatly arranged in diagonal rows, each one marked differently, and together creating exactly

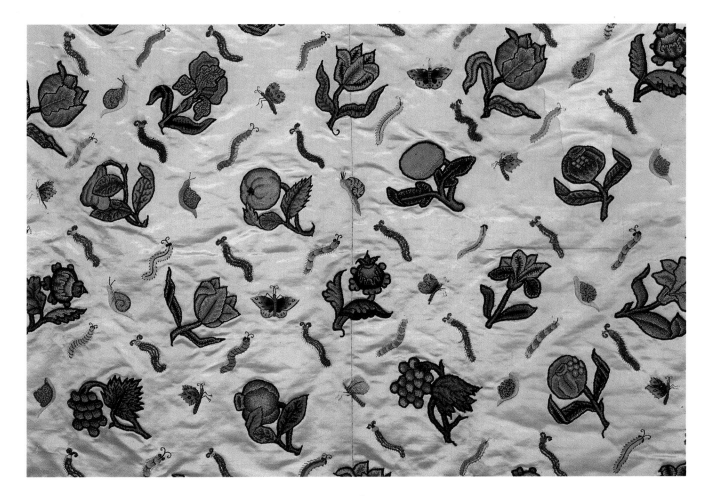

the kind of richly varied effect that appealed so strongly to garden enthusiasts.

Tulips were not grown in solid blocks of colour as they often are in bedding schemes today; they were flowers for connoisseurs and collectors, perfect for creating an eye-catching display, and they were chosen for the fascinating variegation of their petals. 'Nature', as John Gerard noted, seemed 'to play more with this floure than any other', and seventeenth-century embroiderers entered delightedly into the game with as much enthusiasm as the keenest florists. Like them, they ignored the plain-coloured tulips known as 'breeders' and focused their attention on those which had broken into contrasting stripes, recording the different types most faithfully and often depicting them with quantities of small insects. Little did they know that the marks they so admired were the result of a virus infection transferred from one plant to another by aphids! Most of the tulips on the curtain are 'flamed', with a bold central bar up the centre of the petal, but others are 'feathered' with marks running round the petals' edge. And there are examples of bybloemens, which were white with rose and purple markings, and bizarres which were yellow overlaid with shades of red – altogether a mouthwatering collection, and one which is reminiscent of the varieties displayed in the spring garden described by John Rea in *Flora* in 1665:

The *Tulips* to delight your Eyes
With glorious Garments rich and new,
Excelling all in Eden grew;
Like a Rich Glutton some are dight
In Tyrian-purple and fine white;
And in bright Crimson others shine
Impal'd with White and Graydeline:
The meanest here you can behold
Is cloth'd in Scarlet, laced with gold . . .

The poem was addressed to Lady Hanmer, wife of Sir Thomas Hanmer, in whose Flintshire garden the tulip had pride of place. Sir Thomas's *Garden Book* (1653) explains exactly how they should be planted: in beds four foot wide, raised up in the centre 'so that all the flowers may be seen the better'. The tulips were set in ranks, and the most sophisticated colour combinations were planned for each season.

Satin panel c1650 of a lady holding a tulip surrounded by insects and applied flower slips.

(opposite) 'And now the florists fly about' in Belinda Downes' 'Tulipomania (1991) inspired

by Sir Thomas Hanmer's description of new tulips coming into flower. Contemporary stumpwork using mainly couching and straight stitches. The borders are machine embroidered.

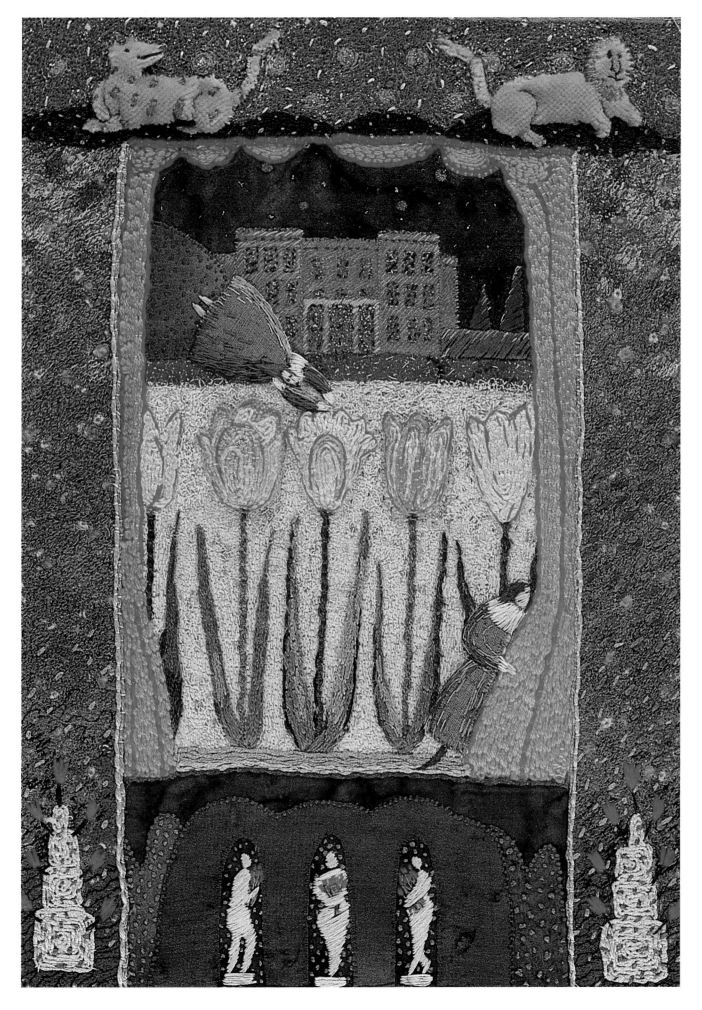

A boy admiring a tulip in a Dutch garden by A. van de Venne, 1623.

There was tremendous excitement when they started to open: 'And now' wrote Sir Thomas, 'the Florists fly about to see and examine and take chief pleasure in gardens, admiring the new varietys that Spring produces.'

The English passion for tulips never quite reached the frenetic heights of the Tulipomania in Holland in the 1630s, when single bulbs changed hands for fortunes, but it was certainly something of a cult. It is fascinating to see how often tulips 'striped, feathered, garded and variously marbled' take the centre of the stage in seventeenth-century needlework, and how ingeniously the embroiderers depicted the variegations of colour.

Stumpwork was a perfect method for rendering the sculptural quality of tulips, but the markings were most accurately conveyed in long and short stitch worked directly on the satin ground. Moreover, could the colourways of flamed and bizarre tulips have inspired some of the striking flame and Hungarian point patterns worked on canvas furnishings during this period, I wonder? The success of these designs depends on sophisticated blending of colours, and some of the most pleasing combine the reds and golds of cultivars like Sir Thomas Hanmer's Amidor, in shades of crimson, yellow and deep red, and Helliodorus in orange, yellow and crimson.

Flamed tulips in Maria Merian's Neues Blumenbuch, *1680.*

PINKS AND CARNATIONS

But what shall I say to the Queene of delight and of flowers, Carnations and Gilloflowers, whose bravery, variety and sweete smell joyned together, tyeth every ones affection with great earnestnesse, both to like and to have them?

John Parkinson, 1629

Both carnations and pinks were known as 'gilliflowers' in Parkinson's day, and the mellifluous name, so redolent of midsummer pleasures, certainly conveys the affection they inspired. Second only to the rose, they endeared themselves to flower enthusiasts as plants to cherish and grow oneself, as well as to admire. 'I have nine or ten several colours, and divers of them as bigge as roses' boasted William Lawson in *The Country Housewife's Garden* (1617), 'of all flowres (save the Damaske Rose) they are the most pleasant to sight and smell: their use is much in ornament . . . '

In needlework their ornamental qualities have made them permanent favourites, and of all the embroiderer's flowers they lend themselves most readily to pattern-making. There is a neatness and precision in their shape not found in roses, and though tulips are equally distinctive in outline, they lack the intricacy of structure that makes the pink an exceptionally versatile as well as decorative motif. The long calyx is a gift to the pattern-drawer, and so are the

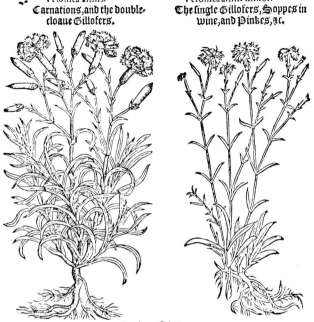

Of Gillofers.   Chap.bij.

The Kyndes.

Vnder the name of Gillofers (at this time) diuerse sortes of floures are contayned. Wherof they call the first the Cloue gillofer whiche in deede is of diuerse sortes & variable colours: the other is the small or singie Gillofer & his kinde. The third is that, which we cal in Englisb sweete williams, & Colminiers: wherevnto we may well iopne the wilde Gillofer or Cockow floure, which is not much vnlike the smaller sort of garden Gillofers.

Vetonica altilis.
Carnations, and the double-cloaue Gillofers.

Vetonica altilis minor.
The single Gillofers, Soppes in wine, and Pinkes, &c.

The Description.

The Cloue gillofer hath long small blades, almost like Leeke blades. The stalke is round, and of a foote and halfe long, full of iopntes and knops, & it beareth

Carnations and pinks were both called gilliflowers, as Henry Lyte's A Nievve Herball *of 1578 makes clear. Pinks, or soppes-in-wine, were used to flavour wines and cordials.*

joints in the stems from which the narrow pointed leaves grow. The plant's natural stiffness makes it a perfect subject for geometrical designs on the counted thread, and it can be seen in countless variations in band patterns and detached motifs in blackwork. Emblematic of love and affection, in betrothal portraits it was often held in the hand or pinned near the face, adding a touch of vibrant colour to contrast with its counterparts embroidered in black and gold on white sleeve ruffles and on ruffs.

'Carnation' in the sixteenth century was the name of a colour as well as a flower – it was a pale red or deep blush, deeper than what we know as 'pink' which was not used as an adjective until two centuries later. But embroiderers also used the word 'pink' to describe the ornamental cutting of slits in a pattern on rich fabrics. The cuts were made with serrated blades similar to those of pinking shears which produced jagged zigzag edges closely resembling the fringed petals of both pinks and carnations; perhaps the flower's name derives from this – certainly it was a feature which translated perfectly in needlework, especially when the flower was treated in a fan shape, as it is on Mary Hulton's cushion on page 37. Mary's pinks with their striking outlines may also have been inspired by the stylised motifs on ceramics and textiles from Persia and Turkey, where these flowers had been grown in gardens long before they were cultivated in England.

The difference between the slight dainty pink (top) and the more robust carnation

(bottom) is shown in this page in Collaert's Florilegium *of 1590.*

DMC pink designs in cross stitch. Note the more decorative effect when the flowers are worked on the diagonal.

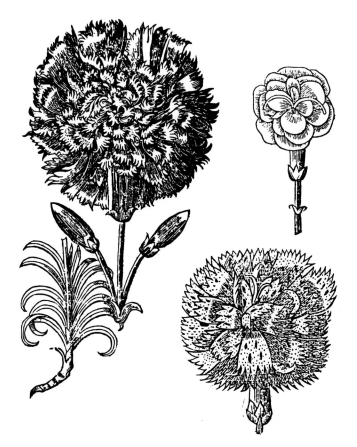

Sixteenth-century Turkish ceramic design from A. H. Christie's Pattern Design.

'Flower in a flower' carnation design from Nature as Ornament by L. F. Day.

The 'Great old Carnation' or 'gray Hulo'; 'Master Tuggie his Princesse'; and (top) 'Master Tuggie his Rose Gilloflower' from Parkinson's Paradisus.

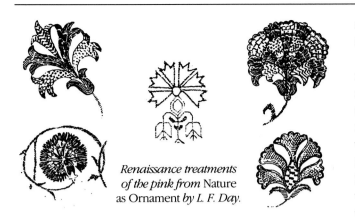

Renaissance treatments of the pink from Nature as Ornament *by L. F. Day.*

describes the luxuriant embroidered versions exploding in silks and crewels on gowns and stomachers.

Carnations were a passion in the eighteenth century, and the success of the florists in raising 'flakes' and 'bizarres', attractively striped in one or more colours was faithfully recorded in embroidery. The florists tried to breed ever more rounded shapes, like 'picotees' which were delicately edged with colour, but these were more difficult to render in stitches, and this may explain why the even more strikingly formalised 'laced' pinks of the nineteenth-century florists were seldom taken up as models by the Berlin designers who continued to offer the fringed varieties.

The fan shapes were ideal for 'flower within a flower' patterns, likewise inspired by Persian and Turkish models, and also for experiments in shading, speckling and streaking, as exciting as any carried out by the hybridists. The 'streaked Gillyflowers' mentioned by Perdita in *A Winter's Tale* were ardently discussed by specialists like Master Tuggie of Westminster, and the streaking and speckling on some of the tent stitch slips (such as on the one illustrated on page 33) suggests that they were worked by an embroiderer who had real models before her. This also seems to have been the case in some seventeenth-century samplers which depict Painted Lady carnations whose petals were red on one side and white on the other, a colour combination ingeniously worked out in needlelace.

The names of old varieties like Parkinson's Ruffling Robin, the Lustie Gallant, and Master Tuggie's rose Gilloflower and Princess exactly suit the jaunty frilled and fringed carnations of stumpwork; just as the two categories of eighteenth-century carnations, one known as 'Bursters' (which, like the nineteenth-century pink named after Mrs Sinkins, split their calyx) and the other as 'Whole Blowers', which aptly

Laced pinks drawn by John Farleigh against a patchwork background in Old Fashioned Flowers.

This stumpwork box c1650 reflects the contemporary delight in flowers. Two ladies, each holding a posy and wearing flower-embroidered dress are depicted with a larger-than-life rose, carnation and tulip whose petals are worked in needlelace.

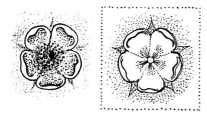

Gwen White's variations on a rose from A World of Pattern *are full of suggestions for stitchery.*

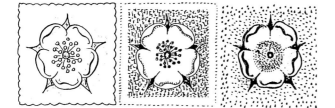

A rose border by Joan Drew.

'A rose is a rose is a rose', wrote Gertrude Stein, seizing the flower's beauty in a single line. But in needlework, each rose reflects the taste and aspirations of its period, and the Glasgow rose is very different from the Tudor rose, and different again from those we embroider today. If you are uncertain which method to choose or how to work out a suitable design, much can be learnt from tracing the treatment of the rose through succeeding periods, seeing how many different techniques can be found, then trying out those which most appeal to you. For example, you might like to make a rose sampler which brings together certain details – of petals, say – in detached buttonhole stitch, laid silks and appliqué; if you experiment with different materials and in a different scale from the originals, their appearance will inevitably be transformed and revitalised.

During the rose season, study the living flowers with the same questioning, analytical eye to see which qualities might transpose in stitchery. For an exercise in tone you might choose *Rosa mutabilis*, whose flowers open cream and gradually fade through shades of pink, deepening to crimson as the petals fall.

Beginners could choose one of the roses pictured on this page as the motif for a simple repeating pattern. In Joan Drew's words: 'It is surprising how workers will often go far afield for elaborate patterns when the simple repetition of one well-drawn flower-form will often give a more delightful effect.'

The original Glasgow rose sketched by Jessie Newbery for an appliqué design.

A cushion cover by Ann Macbeth with roses in satin stitch.

Tulips

Tulip fan (1991), designed and made by Diana Dolman as a wall decoration. The ground is painted silk on a stiffened base, machine embroidered in Madeira 'Sticku' thread using a twelve-year-old Frister and Rossman domestic sewing machine

Restrictions introduced in the 1920s on account of the virus have made the old striped varieties hard to find today, but others equally inspiring for embroiderers are listed in every catalogue. Of these, the slender lily-flowered, cottage and parrot tulips offer some of the most interesting shapes and patterns to explore.

Parrot tulips were considered 'monstrosities' when they first appeared in 1620, but their seductive rococo curves made them favourites in the eighteenth century. Modern embroiderers with a taste for manipulating fabrics would surely find inspiration in the twists and ridges of their irregularly fringed petals and swirling leaves. The veined and marbled leaves of tulips derived from the wild *Tulipa greigii*, in shades of bronze, purple and brown suggest bands of satin stitch of varying width. The subtlety of the leaves contrasts with the brilliance of the scarlet petals, marked at the base with a black zigzag edged in yellow.

There is always a feeling of anticipation when tulips open up in the sunshine: some reveal exciting star shapes, others surprise us with exquisite combinations of colour and pattern created by the dark or pale blotches at the base of the petals. These blotches form a central pool of colour which provides an effective contrast to the indigo or yellowish stamens, picturesquely described by Sir Thomas Hanmer as 'little spears'. They offer marvellous ready-made designs and colour schemes, just waiting to be transposed into stitchery.

Eirian Short's 'Tulips', 1989, conveys the sculptural quality of the flowers. It is worked in crewel wools, mixing up to three colours in the needle in directional straight stitches 'as a painter puts in brushstrokes'. The ground is a firm Welsh flannel.

(above) *'The Tulip Border' by Wendy Brown, 1989, hand embroidery on painted silk, in which straight stitches are used to bring out the leaf patterns.*

The decorative shapes of tulips are emphasised in Studies in Plant Form and Design *(1895).*

(left) *Tulip design in laid work from* Embroidery *(1909).*

(far left) Tulipa Eichleri, *'which drew every visitor towards it with magnetic certainty', illustrated by Evelyn Dunbar in* Gardener's Choice *(1937).*

PINKS AND CARNATIONS

The old designs are particularly rich in possibilities for today. The irresistible frilling and speckling of the carnations in Sweert's *Florilegium* come to life again in Sue Rangeley's dress embroidery (see p156), where machine edging curls the petals extravagantly; and the exaggerated shapes in *Studies in Plant Form and Design* ask to be tried out in appliqué and Assisi work. In *Embroidery and Tapestry Weaving* Grace Christie emphasises the shape of the carnation in her diagrams, showing how the right choice of stitch can help bring out the character of the plant as well.

Then, too, there are phrases in the old garden books which set the embroiderer's mind racing: 'Carnation Gilloflowers for beauty . . . deserve letters of gold' wrote Stephen Blake in *The Complete Gardener's Practice* in 1664 – urging you to try out the flower writing on page 118, or the carnation motifs and initials on page 122. He went on to list his favourites, among them the 'Patern of Nature'. Was the name of this, like the Embroidered Cranesbill, perhaps inspired by flowers seen in needlework? I would like to think so, and when time permits I shall search out some further mention or illustration of it; and if none comes to light I shall make up my own 'Patern of Nature', turning for inspiration to the florilegia whose pages are reproduced in this book, and to the gilliflowers most resembling the old varieties that I cosset and cherish in my own garden.

(right) *Ornamental treatment of pinks from* Studies in Plant Form and Design.

Stitches for carnations from Embroidery and Tapestry Weaving: *(a) cretan stitch, (b) herring bone or double back stitch, (c) gradual shading in satin stitch worked in a chevron pattern.*

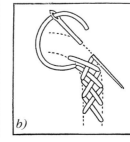

a)   *b)*   *c)*

Carnation dress and sleeve trimming by Sue Rangeley (1991) using hand-painted silk organza mounted in a hoop and machine satin stitched in fine metallic threads. When released from the tension of the hoop, the close machining curled the petal edges automatically.

A page of spotted, striped and feathered carnations in Sweert's Florilegium *(1612).*

A PLEA FOR THE FUTURE

Searching for the illustrations in this book took me to libraries, museums and houses all over Britain and abroad, and gave me immense pleasure in the process. The choice in fact was far wider than I had ever imagined, making the final selection exceedingly difficult. It was governed partly by the availability of photographs, and partly by the personal factor – the interest, or appeal, or simple curiosity which the work of one or another embroiderer (past or present) aroused in me. For example, although Jane Allgood's chair cover is faded, her portrait still reveals its original brilliance, together with her pride in her work and her determination to have it recorded; Lady Ottoline Morrell's description of the making of her bedspread certainly contributes to our interest in it; and Mrs Delany's passion for flowers and for recording them in needlework illuminates her writing.

Yet beside these examples, alas! how many embroiderers from the past are but shadowy figures – and this will continue to be the case today and tomorrow, unless *we* choose to change it. To add a date and your name is essential; but how much more interesting would it be, to tell also how long the work took, and what inspired it! This postscript is called 'A plea for the future' in the hope that you might follow Mrs Morrell's example and keep a written record of your embroidery. It could be a list like hers, describing the design of each piece and giving the recipient's name, or a sort of scrapbook which might include preparatory sketches and also photographs of the completed work with your comments on its making and the finished result.

Such a record surely merits an embroidered cover of a most personal kind. I hope you might find inspiration for it in the flowers in this book, interpreting them in your own way in the colours and methods that please you most, uninfluenced by current fads and fancies. In the words of Richard Hatton:

> We have to trust our own choice after all, and end with the simple belief that what pleases us is beautiful. Indeed, no other rule is of any use to us, and if we do but honestly please ourselves, and make forms which genuinely give us pleasure, we shall find ourselves credited with the power of designing beautiful things.

'Narcissus in a Chinese Mug' by the author, 1987. The long shape was inspired by a Spanish 'bodegon' or still-life painting by Francisco de Zurbaran, and the method, using appliqué in felt, by eighteenth-century flower pictures. The ground is drugget, and the narcissus is in machine whip stitch.

157

INDEX

Panel designed by Ann Macbeth, for Miss Cranston's famous Tea Rooms in Glasgow, illustrated in The Studio *in 1903.*

Carnation from Maria Merian's Neues Blumenbuch.

BIBLIOGRAPHY

GENERAL INTEREST

Arnold, Janet *The Secrets of Queen Elizabeth's Wardrobe Unlocked* (W. S. Maney, 1987)
Ashelford, Jane *Dress in the Age of Queen Elizabeth* (Batsford, 1988)
Blunt, Wilfred *The Art of Botanical Illustration* (Collins, 1971)
Coats, Alice *The Treasury of Flowers* (Phaidon, 1975)
Duthie, Ruth *Florists' Flowers and Societies* (Shire, 1988)
Hayden, Ruth *Mrs Delany: Her life and her flowers* (British Museum Publications, 1980)

FLOWER BOOKS

These books are of special interest to embroiderers as a source of patterns. This list includes only modern reprints and selections. Many of the originals mentioned in the text may be consulted in the National Art Library of the Victoria and Albert Museum (open to the public) and the Lindley Library of the Royal Horticultural Society (members only).
De Passe, Crispin *Hortus Floridus* (1615) (Minerva Press, 1974)
Hatton, Richard *The Handbook of Plant and Floral Ornament* (Dover, 1960) (first published as *The Craftman's Plant-Book*, 1909)
Le Moyne de Morgues, Jacques *The Work of Jacques Le Moyne de Morgues* ed Paul Hulton (British Museum Publications, 1977)
Merian, Maria Sybilla *The Wondrous Transformation of Caterpillars* (Scholar Press, 1978). Fifty engravings selected from *Erucarum Ortis* (1718)
Sweerts, Emanuel *Early Floral Engravings* (Dover, 1976). 110 plates from the 1612 *Florilegium*

EMBROIDERY BOOKS

Christie, Mrs Archibald *Samplers and Stitches* (1920) (Batsford, 1989)
Harker, Gail *Machine Embroidery* (Merehurst, 1989)
Hirst, Barbara and Roy *Raised Embroidery: exploring decorative Stumpwork* (Merehurst, 1992)
Lemon, Jane *Embroidered Boxes* (Batsford, 1989) Making practical items for embroidery, including detailed instructions for book covers, bags and cushions

ACKNOWLEDGEMENTS

This book is made by its illustrations, and I must begin by thanking all the owners of historic needlework and the embroiderers whose work is reproduced. Then I would like to thank Paddy Killer for devising such witty chapter headings, Sarah Siddall for making elegant line drawings from faded photographs and photocopies, and Ruth Duthie and Mary Grierson for helping me to identify needlework flowers. I am also much indebted to Doctor Brent Elliott, Ruth Hayden, Lorna Rogerson, Lanto Synge and Frank Villaz; and at David & Charles to my editor Vivienne Wells and in particular to Sue Cleave who made decorative sense of a most unwieldy mass of material.

COLOUR ILLUSTRATIONS

Agecroft Association, Richmond, Virginia p65; The Marquess of Bath p46; Bodleian Library, Oxford p141; Bowes Museum, Barnard Castle p38; Bridgeman Art Library p8; collection of the Duke of Buccleuch and Queensberry p16; Christies, London p18 (left and right); Frances Dower photo p1; collection Doxiadis p91; Alan Duns photos pp63, 119, 138; Embroiderers' Guild pp50, 52; English Heritage p10; Mark Fiennes photos p45 (left and right); Fine Art Society, London p144; Glasgow Museums and Galleries pp71, 111, 113; Holburne Museum, Bath p151; P. Johnstone photo p24 (bottom); Mallett, London pp5, 41, 143 (top); Musée de Cluny, cliché des Musées Nationaux p6; Museum of Art, Rhode Island School of Design (gift of Lucy Aldrich) p67; Museums and Galleries on Merseyside p48; Jim Pascoe photos pp106, 136, 153; The Principal, Fellows and Scholars of Jesus College, Oxford p114; Eddie Ryle-Hodges photo p100; in a Scottish collection, photo J. Forsyth p97; Spink, London pp127, 131; Patrick Stable photo p27 (top); Tate Gallery p108; C. Thacker photos pp27 (right), 57, 59, 82, 105, 120, 123, 143 (bottom); Trustees of the National Museums of Scotland p39; Victoria and Albert Museum pp20, 98, 145, photos C. Bishop pp33 (right), 51, 61, 78, 81, 98, 112, 133, 145; Mrs Margaret Whytehead p77. The following are in private collections: pp14, 26, 33 (left), 35, 59 (left), 68 (top), 75, 82, 83, 100, 120, 153.

BLACK & WHITE ILLUSTRATIONS

The Archives, Birmingham Institute of Art and Design p134; Ashmolean Museum, Oxford p53 (bottom); Bibliothèque Albert I, Brussels, p74 (bottom); Bibliothèque du Museum d'Histoire Naturelle, Paris pp72 (top), 128 (bottom); British Library pp9, 41 (bottom), 68 (bottom left), 80 (top and centre), 129 (top), 149 (bottom); British Museum p40 (bottom); The Earl of Crawford and Balcarres p47 (bottom); Folger Shakespeare Library, Washington pp11, 127, 142 (centre); Glasgow Museums and Art Galleries pp55, 152 (bottom), 159; Paddy Killer chapter headings pp10, 32, 60, 108, 126, 141; Lindley Library, Royal Horticultural Society p118 (top right); Metropolitan Museum of Art, New York pp35, 42, 146; John Murray pp85, 152; R. W. Neugebauer p13; Mary Rhodes p45; Rijkmuseum, Amsterdam p148 (top); Sarah Siddall pp12, 17, 18, 21 (right), 22 (top), 23 (top), 37, 40 (top), 43, 70 (top), 94 (bottom), 109 (top), 125 (centre and bottom right); Southampton City Art Gallery p21; C. Thacker p98; Victoria and Albert Museum pp25 (top), 37 (top), 64, 118 (top left), photos C. Bishop pp90, 101 (top); Whitworth Art Gallery, Manchester p73 (top); William Morris Gallery, Walthamstow pp102, 144. The following are in private collections; pp19, 26, 44, 49, 69 (top), 71 (bottom), 72 (bottom), 76, 79, 88 (left), 93 (top), 95, 99, 106, 116, 117 (right), 130, 132, 137, 142 (bottom), 148 (bottom), 149 (top).

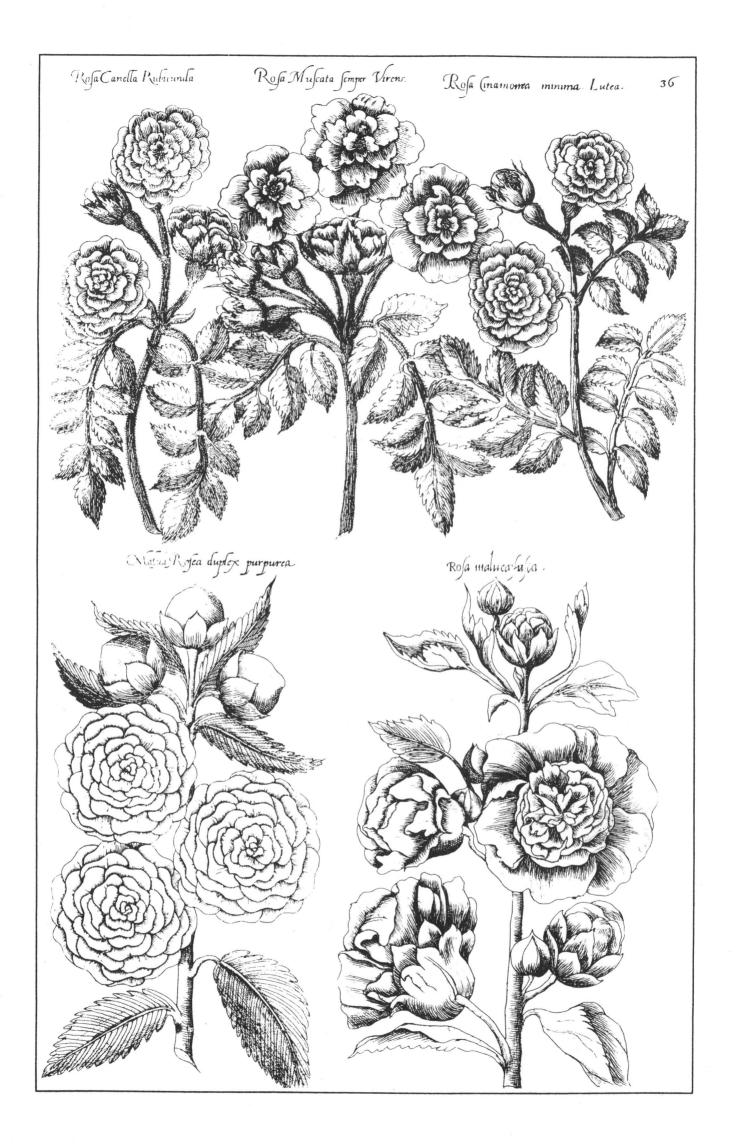

RofaCanella Rubicunda   Rofa Mufcata femper Virens.   Rofa Cinamoma minima Lutea.   36

Mafia Rofea duplex purpurea   Rofa malucahufea.